Content packaged by Mojo Media, Inc.
Editor: Joe Funk
Creative Director: Jason Hinman

ISBN: 1-57243-796-0
ISBN 13: 978-1-57243-796-8

This book is available in quantity at special discounts for your group or organization.
For further information, contact:

Triumph Books
601 S. LaSalle St.
Suite 500
Chicago, Illinois 60605
Phone: (312) 939-3330
Fax: (312) 663-3557

Printed in the United States of America

Contents

Eyes On The Prize

Can't-miss Illinois kids put on a heck of a show

By Mike Downey

Well, I give up.

I can't even choose the most amazing thing about the Illinois Fighting Illini anymore.

That they are 28-0?

That none of these 28 games has been closer than five points?

That they have used the same starting five for all 28?

That they have been the No. 1 team in America for 12 weeks?

That they could lose a game now and probably still be ranked No. 1?

Something quite startling is happening here in Champaign-Urbana.

Illinois is doing more than just winning. It is taking no prisoners.

Northwestern never knew what hit it Wednesday night. An 84-48 loss was the worst beating any opponent has handed the Wildcats since 1998.

Ten days ago, Northwestern's basketball opponent was Texas A&M-Corpus Christi.

The Wildcats won by eight.

Wednesday's opponent was, uh, not Texas A&M-Corpus Christi.

The Wildcats did not win by eight. To lose by eight would have been a blessing.

They fell behind 9-1, then 21-9, then 42-17.

Asked for an opening statement after a 36-point loss, Northwestern's coach, Bill Carmody, said that at one point early in the game, "We're down 7-0 and we still haven't got a shot off.

"From there, it just got worse. That's my statement."

Illinois nailed 14 three-point shots. Northwestern nailed only 22 shots all night ... from anywhere.

Dee Brown racked 'em up from all over Assembly Hall, usually while Wildcats watched him from a safe distance.

They were H-O-R-S-E shots, Brown said. Just pick a spot on the floor, aim and fire.

Somebody asked, "Did you have a

hand in your face on any of your three-pointers?"

"That's a good question," Brown said.

The Illini popped from long range. And they also alley-ooped passes for dunks. And they also passed the ball expertly. They did everything a good - no, great - college basketball team is supposed to do.

Brown said he remembered 10 or 11 crisp passes on one possession alone. Around and around the ball went - the kind of textbook stuff coaches dream about.

"That was the best ball movement I ever saw in my life," Brown said.

Other times, the Illini just let it fly.

They defy explanation. They transcend superlatives. Their record is now 25-0 in games in which they hold a lead at the half. (They are 47-2 in this respect since Bruce Weber became head coach.)

They have won 20 in a row at home. They have won 24 of 28 by margins of double figures. They are running out of records and streaks and stretches to count.

And yet supposedly Somebody Out There still says Illinois is not the No. 1 team in the land?

"I don't know ... who says that?" Carmody asked. "Wasn't that like five weeks ago? I don't hear people say it so much as I hear people say that they're saying it."

The Illini are running out of goals before the NCAA tournament can begin. A piece of the Big Ten title already is theirs. Roger Powell even got an assist ... his first in a conference game in 333 minutes on the court.

They have won 28 games. Just one Illinois team won more ... the 31-game winners who made it to the 1989 Final Four.

And it isn't even March.

"We're not celebrating," Brown said. "We're waiting."

Even that, this team is doing right.

Brown is the man making Illinois click

By Vahe Gregorian

The essential dynamics of this mesmerizing University of Illinois basketball team seem infinite. Without any one aspect of its character, its DNA, the Illini would be just another contender.

Here is their gravel-voiced, gregarious coach, Bruce Weber, who slogged along in relative anonymity for 18 years as a Purdue assistant before at last getting to run his own program at Southern Illinois University Carbondale.

Five years later, all dues suddenly accounted for, he inherited an Illinois team bursting with talent but disinclined to embrace him - yet molded it into the very vision of what a team should be.

Here are forwards James Augustine and Roger Powell Jr., backed by Jack Ingram and Nick Smith, supposedly the weak link or trap door that ultimately will dash an otherwise promising team's hopes.

Twenty-eight undefeated games into the season, after Wednesday night's 84-48 pulping of Northwestern, that apparent inevitability has yet to successfully be exploited by any Illini foe.

And then we come to the so-called three-headed monster, guards Dee Brown, Luther Head and Deron Williams.

Each would make a deserving Big Ten player of the year, and national player of the year. Each has been crucial to Illinois' remarkable run and ambitions of reaching the NCAA Tournament Final Four in St. Louis.

But for all the vital elements Head and Williams provide the Illini, as indispensable as the rest of the team is, one player still is more indispensable than the rest:

Game after game, day after day, moment by moment, Brown is the face, aura, catalyst, starter, finisher and soul of this team.

Everything from tempo to temperament stems from Brown.

"We live off his energy," Weber said.

Though Weber is careful to spread praise around and reluctant to proclaim one player the key, take Brown away and it simply would not be the same

him was so bewildered that he stopped, shrugged and seemed to be saying, "What am I supposed to do?"

But perhaps the most devastating 3 of the sequence was the last, which Brown launched from more than 25 feet away. Seconds later, he was scampering in for a breakaway layup off a Rich McBride pass.

For good measure, Brown added another 3 just before the half, leaving even Weber not knowing what to do other than sit and clap.

The series of events would be noteworthy enough if it were an isolated contribution by one player to one Illini victory. But making such commotion is Brown's trademark, and he is only becoming more refined.

team. A very good team, yes, but not one on trajectory to win the school's first men's basketball title.

The Illini could ill-afford to lose any other player, for that matter, but Brown is the one who gives the Illini their zest and oomph and strut and, finally, their advantage. Williams called him the guy who "gets us going on the defensive end and the offensive end."

"I see him every day, and every day it's still amazing to see how fast he actually moves when he gets out there," Ingram said, adding, "He always brings me something new that I've never seen before from him."

The farce at Assembly Hall on Wednesday represented a microcosm of Brown's typical impact.

Whisking in three 3-pointers in less than five minutes, Brown scored 14 of the Illini's first 28 points as they took a 13-point lead that ballooned from there.

The second of the 3s came at the end of a dizzying half-court passing sequence by the Illini, who Brown estimated made 14 passes in the span. Like a pinball or video game, Weber called it.

"That was the best ball movement I ever saw in my life," said Brown, who said the Northwestern defender nearest

"Dee Brown came into this league as a slasher . . . wasn't much of a shooter," Northwestern coach Bill Carmody said. "Now two-thirds of the shots Dee Brown takes are 3-point shots. He doesn't go to the rim like he did-not that he couldn't."

For the night, Brown made six of eight 3s, leaving him shooting .468 (72 of 154) from 3-point range this season. He added the obligatory five assists and two steals, and the Illini were 28-0.

"It's hard to be Dee Brown; it's hard to live up to being Dee Brown," Weber said, adding, "As of late, he's been pretty special."

© 2005, St. Louis Post-Dispatch.
Distributed by Knight Ridder/Tribune Information Services.

The Season

The Season

A game by game summary of the Fighting Illini's Dream Season

NOVEMBER 19:
ILLINOIS 87, DELAWARE STATE 67

You gotta start somewhere, right? Before the 2004-05 Fighting Illini could become a juggernaut, they had to win a game. And before they could become the country's top-ranked team in The Associated Press poll, they had to claw up from No. 6.

Playing lowly Delaware State in the opener was a good way to test the waters, although those waters were surprisingly rough in the early going. At one point, the Illini even were trailing by five points, 9-4.

But then the mighty Fighting Illini machine began to rumble forward, much to the delight of the Orange-clad masses at Assembly Hall. And the player at the controls was Dee Brown, a junior guard. Brown was the Illini's most exciting player in 2003-04, averaging 13.3 points per game and earning Second-Team All-Big Ten honors.

Thanks to his work against Delaware State, the Illini had a commanding 50-37 lead by halftime. With the Illini losing 28-27 with 6:45 remaining in the first half, Brown rattled off five straight points, including a three-pointer, to set his team in motion. That half, Brown had 11 points and was 3-for-3 from three-point range.

Brown simply was glad to be playing in a game following weeks of practice. "The games are everything," Brown said. "I love playing basketball."

Of course, the Illini were the very definition of the word "team," so Brown didn't power them all by himself. Although he finished the game with a team-high 17 points, he was closely followed by fellow guard Luther Head (15 points) and Deron Williams (12 points). And the big man on the boards was 6-10, 230-pound junior James Augustine, who led Illinois with seven rebounds and also pitched in 15 points.

It turned out to be the dominant win everyone had expected, but Illinois wasn't satisfied. The team had bigger goals for the season than beating up on also-rans like Delaware State. Much bigger goals.

"They made us go to sleep a little bit," said Head, a senior leader. "They just exploited by penetrating. Tonight we had a bad defensive game."

But things only would get better from here. Remember, you gotta start somewhere.

NOVEMBER 21:
ILLINOIS 91, FLORIDA A&M 60

This was another small step on the road to glory. Actually, it was microscopic. Florida A&M's was unranked like Delaware State, and it didn't figure to improve its status in an intimidating place like Assembly Hall.

The high point for Florida A&M was jumping out to a 2-0 lead. Then the game got ugly in a hurry. First Augustine sank two free throws; then Head nailed a three-point jump shot; then Brown cruised in for a layup; then Brown made a three-pointer; then Williams followed with a three-pointer of his own; then Augustine brought the crowd to its feet with a thunderous dunk; and then Augustine hit two free throws. When the dust settled, the Fighting Illini were winning 19-2. By the half, Illinois had opened a ridiculous 58-29 advantage.

And the man at the controls? Brown, of course. The 6-0, 185-pound guard was 8-of-8 from the field, including four three-pointers. "He's come out and just played with such energy and shot the ball so well," Illinois coach Bruce Weber said. "That little stretch—for a little guy, he dominated the game pretty convincingly."

After that first half, however, Brown's work was done.

He let his teammates take over while he attempted just two shots the rest of the game.

Those teammates had no problem adjusting to the glare of the bright lights. All told, five Illini players finished in double digits in scoring. In addition to Brown (a team-leading 20 points), senior forward Roger Powell Jr. (15), Head (13), Williams (11) and Augustine (10) scored pretty much at will. The win was so overwhelming that the Illini were afforded the opportunity to empty their bench; sophomore forward Warren Carter and freshman forward Shaun Pruitt had eight and seven points, respectively, and senior center Nick Smith contributed six rebounds.

It seemed like a flawless win, but in the eyes of Weber, there was room for improvement. In his never-ending quest to push his team toward perfection, he focused on a point in the second half when Florida A&M rallied briefly and mounted a 15-4 run to cut the Illini lead to 62-46. It was by no means a tense moment for Illinois, but Weber was looking for any type of motivator he could find.

"We had 15 possessions, one basket, and nine turnovers in that stretch," said coach. "It wasn't very good basketball."

In a way, Weber was right. The Illini could get away with mistakes against teams like Delaware State and Florida A&M, but the future would be less forgiving.

NOVEMBER 24:
ILLINOIS 85, OAKLAND 54

Before those tests arrived, however, the Illini were presented with another easy target. Not much from this matchup would wind up in their scrapbook.

The weather certainly didn't help to create a big-game atmosphere. Many fans were scared off by a brutal snowstorm in Champaign, so Assembly Hall was unusually subdued. Then there was the little matter of the Illini's opponent. Oakland had an 0-1 record—and no betting man in his right mind would have taken the Golden Grizzlies here.

Head, a senior, was the one who stepped up on this night, putting together his first great game of the season. Head scored all of the Illini's first seven points as they jumped out to a 7-2 lead in the first two minutes.

And once Head's teammates got involved, Oakland had absolutely no chance. The Illini's work from the perimeter was typically outstanding throughout the first half, especially from three-point range. Illinois hit nine three-pointers, with Head accounting for an amazing five of them.

The second half brought more of the same, as the Illini hit a variety of perimeter shots, including three more three-pointers. All told, Illinois was 12-for-24 from three-point range. Head was undeniably the star of the show—he had 22 points, a career-best six three-pointers, nine assists, and two steals—but as usual, the Illini spread the wealth. Williams and Powell also scored in double digits, with 17 and 10 points, respectively, and a deep bench added 22 total points.

Despite winning another game in dominant fashion, the Illini weren't yet close to being perfect. Not according to Weber, anyway. He was fixated on the team's less-than-stellar ball-handling, which resulted in 16 turnovers. "I think we're still a little sloppy with the basketball," he said. "I want them to take care of the ball."

Once again, Weber had a valid point. While the Illini's average margin of victory in the opening three games had been a whopping 27.3 points, that number was deceptive. Neither Delaware State, Florida A&M, nor Oakland was a big-time team, so these had been little more than exhibition games. The Illini were 3-0 and had moved up in the national rankings to No. 5, but they still had no idea how good they really were.

NOVEMBER 27:
ILLINOIS 89, GONZAGA 72

This was the game everyone had been anticipating. It would, well, tell Illinois exactly how good it was. Gonzaga was the Illini's first topflight opponent—it was ranked 24th in the country. The Bulldogs had a way of living up to their nickname. They often were at their fiercest on college basketball's grandest stages. In recent years, they had provided some of the most memorable moments in the NCAA Tournament, scoring major upsets.

This wasn't the NCAA Tournament, but it was a pretty big stage nonetheless. The game would take place in the John Wooden Tradition at Conseco Fieldhouse in Indianapolis? It was a tournament named after a legend, played in a state with a rich basketball tradition.

The matchup had the feel of a heavyweight prizefight, and Illinois delivered the knockout punch early. The key was to neutralize Ronny Turiaf, a 6-10, 249-pound senior forward who had scored 40 points in Gonzaga's victory over Idaho three days earlier. The Illini did exactly what they wanted to do against Turiaf. Although he had nine points, he turned the ball over six times.

Gonzaga had no answers for the Illini, whose defense was relentless. They forced 19 turnovers and blocked six shots, three of which came from Augustine.

"We were thoroughly dominated today in every phase of the game," Gonzaga coach Mark Few said. "There were times it didn't appear we belonged on the court."

That was exactly how the Illini had planned it. There was no way they were going to let this golden opportunity slip through their fingers. Said Williams, "We just came out and tried to make a statement, show we're for real."

If there were any doubts before the game started, there weren't after the first five minutes. Fueled by seven points from Williams and five from Head, they jumped out to an 18-4 advantage. By halftime, the Illini had stretched their lead to 58-27.

In that pivotal first half, the Illini shot 55 percent from the field and nailed 10 of 17 three-point attempts. They finished the game with 14 three-pointers in 28 tries, including five from Williams, four from Head, and three from Brown.

"We shoot the ball so well and with such confidence," Head said. "Once we start making shots, it's going to be a long night for the other team."

The reserve players also contributed mightily to the cause, which boded well for the rest of the season. They pounded the boards all game long, coming up with 14 rebounds, including five from Smith and four apiece from senior forward/center Jack Ingram and sophomore forward Warren Carter.

The team's performance was so commanding across the board that Weber—brace yourself—was beaming afterward. Try as he might, he couldn't find fault with his players in what was their most important game of the young season.

"This is the kind of game you're going to play in the Sweet 16 or Elite Eight," Weber said. "Can you compete? Anything like this is going to help us down the road."

It was a huge win, to be sure. But the Illini quickly put it behind them. After all, an even tougher team was just ahead on the schedule.

DECEMBER 1: ILLINOIS 91, WAKE FOREST 73

The Fighting Illini still were an impressive fifth in the national rankings, but there was no guarantee they'd stay there long. Next up was mighty Wake Forest, which was the No. 1 team. Illinois fans approached this game with understandable trepidation. After all, history said their beloved team would lose. The Illini were 1-19 against top-ranked teams and hadn't beaten one since their 57-55 victory over Michigan State way back in 1979.

But there was at least one reason to believe things would be different this time around: That lone victory had come at Assembly Hall, and as fate would have it, this game against Wake Forest would be played in those same friendly confines. Apparently, a little home cooking was all the Illini needed.

Like the game against Gonzaga, Illinois wasted no time getting started, mounting a 17-10 lead in the first five minutes behind five points from Powell and four from Head. Seven minutes later Illinois was up 33-20, and it led 54-33 at the half.

For all intents and purposes, that was the ballgame.

The second half was wasn't even a competition—it was a showcase for Illinois basketball. There were more dunks and more three-pointers, and there was more stifling defense. At one point, the Illini stretched their lead to 32 points.

The victory was more resounding than even the most optimistic Illini supporters could have hoped for. And in humbling Wake Forest, Illinois showed it could overcome adversity. Williams played sparingly in the tone-setting first half due to foul trouble, and he finished the game with only eight points. But the other four starters—Powell, Head, Brown and Augustine—picked up the slack with 19, 16, 16 and 10 points, respectively.

"Playing without Deron is tough," Brown said. "He's a great asset to our team, but when he goes out, someone else has got to step up. I think Luther and Roger and myself made some shots and played hard."

The Fighting Illini really were rolling now. These nuggets said it all:

• They never trailed Wake Forest, which was par for

the course. In their five games, which spanned 200 minutes, they had played from behind for fewer than eight total minutes.

• They continued to play suffocating defense. Wake Forest's two most explosive players, Chris Paul and Justin Gray, were limited to 10 and 11 points, respectively.

• They had a season-low six turnovers against Wake Forest, so true to Weber's wishes, they were starting to take care of the basketball.

The Illini still weren't No. 1—they were elevated to No. 3 after beating Wake Forest—but no one doubted they were on their way. This would be remembered as the biggest victory of the entire regular season, one that made the players, coaches and fans believe that anything was possible.

DECEMBER 4:
ILLINOIS 72, ARKANSAS 60

Of course, among the possibilities was a letdown. That was what Weber feared most. After soaring to such amazing heights with the victory over Wake Forest, the Illini were bound to be flat-footed the next time out.

And they couldn't afford to play a shoddy game against the Razorbacks, who no longer were national-title contenders but still could hold their own. They entered the game with a 5-0 record, and the perfect way to add even more juice to their season was to upset the nation's hottest team.

Arkansas set out to play a physical brand of basketball against the Illini, and its plan worked. For the first time all season, Illinois had difficulty finding the open shots. Still, the team hung tough and managed to build a 40-31 lead by the half.

"They came out and tried to force turnovers," Williams said. "It was definitely the most pressure we have had all year."

The second half brought more pressure. In fact, Arkansas narrowed the Illini's lead to 57-53 with about eight minutes remaining. Lesser teams may have folded, but Illinois rose to the challenge. Thanks to some solid free-throw shooting down the stretch, Weber's troops put away pesky Arkansas.

Compared to the season's previous games, the final numbers weren't pretty. The Illini turned the ball over 14 times and shot just 36.5 percent from the field.

Furthermore, they converted on just 5 of 16 three-point attempts. Had it not been for Powell, the final outcome of the game might have been much different. The forward played perhaps his best basketball of the season, leading the team with 19 points and 11 rebounds.

But the numbers were inconsequential in this one. In beating Arkansas, the Illini showed Weber something a stat sheet never could reveal: heart. The heart of a champion.

"I'm proud of us," Weber said. "We didn't play pretty, and the stats aren't pretty. I'm happy we didn't wear down physically."

No, this team wasn't about to wear down. It was getting stronger each day.

DECEMBER 6:
ILLINOIS 78, CHICAGO STATE 59

Chicago State was a second-tier team with an 0-4 record, so why was Assembly Hall rocking like there was no tomorrow when the two teams took the floor? Because this was a monumental moment in the season. Earlier in the day, the Illini had been christened No. 1 in the AP poll. It was only the third time in school history the program had reached such heights (it also happened in 1952 and 1989).

The players, though, weren't in a mood to swing from the rafters. They simply took things in stride. "We didn't jump for joy or anything like that," Head said of his team's reaction to the No. 1 ranking. "We just took it like, 'OK, we're No. 1. Now let's stay there.'"

First they had to stay awake. Perhaps the Illini were a little too ho-hum about their new status. Much to the chagrin of Weber, his team didn't put forth its best effort.

"Sometimes you kind of fall asleep on the court a little bit," Powell said, noting that Chicago State's strategy was to slow the tempo of the game. "I think that's what made it seem like we didn't get up for it. It was a real slow game."

Luckily, the Illini didn't need to be in prime form to defeat Chicago State. Within three minutes, the Illini were winning 8-2; within 10 minutes, they were up 23-13; and by the half, the lead was a comfortable 45-32. From there, Illinois simply focused on keeping its overmatched foe at an arm's length.

But afterward inside the locker room, the Illini players knew they would need to turn it up a notch to remain the

top team in the nation. The 18 turnovers they had committed against Chicago State, as well as their frightful 62.5 shooting percentage from the free-throw line, just wouldn't cut it in the future.

"Everybody will get up for us," said Brown. "It's going to be tough, but that's what makes those games fun."

The fun was just beginning.

DECEMBER 9:
ILLINOIS 74, GEORGETOWN 59

Historically, the No. 1 ranking had been a curse for the Illini. The program's other two reigns as the top team in the country had lasted just one game.

Did the same fate await? Were the Illini doomed? If Georgetown had its way, they were. Like Arkansas, Georgetown had seen better days, but at 3-1, it was a formidable opponent, especially on its home turf. The Hoyas hadn't beaten a top-ranked team since 1985, so they had a chance to make little history of their own.

And for a few flickering moments, it looked as if they might succeed. The Illini had made a habit of burying their opponents early, but on this night, that strategy was stymied. The Hoyas matched Illinois shot for shot. Actually, they did better than that. They put Illinois in its biggest hole of the season, leading for 11:20 of the first half.

The reason for this sudden change in fortune? The Illini's signature three-pointers all but dried up. Illinois made just one three-pointer in the opening half, courtesy of Brown, who hit it in the first minute of play. The Illini, however, were a crafty bunch. "Today [the three-pointers] weren't going," Weber said. "We had to chill out."

But the Illini were a resourceful group. They simply moved into the paint and started throwing their elbows around. "That's the key to our team," Powell said. "We have guys who can score outside, guys who can score inside. And when someone's not on, we've got to step up and make some baskets."

The Illini stepped up all right. They opened a 43-28 lead with 16:44 remaining and never let Georgetown back in the game. Although Illinois finished with a season-low five three-pointers, the results were essentially the same: a double-digit victory. It was the team's eighth double-digit win in as many tries.

The Illini had learned a valuable lesson in this win:

They weren't just a bunch of perimeter shooters. And yes, they still were No. 1.

DECEMBER 11:
ILLINOIS 83, OREGON 66

The Illini were impervious to the pressure of being the hunted. Heading into their matchup against Oregon, which took place in front of thousands of alumni at the United Center in Chicago, they seemed as loose as ever. These guys weren't tight—on the contrary, they were enjoying their time in the limelight.

"I don't think it's any pressure," Weber said of the No. 1 ranking. "It's fun we're up there. We knew we were going to be one of the top teams, and I think they want to hold on to it as long as they can."

Oregon, of course, had a say in that. It was undefeated (4-0) and wanted to do everything it could to prove it belonged on the same court with the Illini. That was Oregon's plan, anyway—but it didn't work. Very simply, the Ducks got blown out of the water.

Using their standard combination of confounding defense, selfless passing and pinpoint shooting, the Illini settled the issue early. By halftime they were up by 14 points, a lead they stretched to 21 at one juncture in the second half.

Like every other coach who had been charged with stopping the Illini this season, Oregon's Ernie Kent was left to shake his head in disbelief afterward. "If you have any type of slippage whatsoever, they really make you pay," Kent said. "They've got a chance to have a special year."

Head was the catalyst this time, scoring a season-best 23 points and going 8-for-10 from the field. But the Illini weren't a one-man show, a two-man two, a three-man show, or even a four-man show. They were a five-man show, particularly against Oregon. Every starter scored at least 10 points, the second time that had happened in 2004-05. In addition to Head's team-best total, Williams had 17 points, Brown had 13, Powell had 12 and Augustine had 10. It was little wonder, then, that the Illini as a whole shot 58 percent from the field and 86.4 percent from the foul line.

The scary thing was, the Illini hadn't even reached their peak yet. They figured they still had a whole lot of growing left to do.

"We're just worried about getting better and preparing for each game as it comes to us," Williams said. "Hopefully, we can keep that ranking for a little longer."

Or maybe even a lot longer.

DECEMBER 19:
ILLINOIS 93, VALPARAISO 56

Weber didn't even bother to try to persuade his team that it would need to be firing on all cylinders to win this game. No one would have believed him.

Valparaiso was an overachieving program that had produced several outstanding seasons in the past decade. But this year had been a real downer for the Crusaders. They staggered into Assembly Hall on this Sunday afternoon with a 2-5 record.

So knowing there basically was no way the Illini could lose, Weber issued a different kind of challenge. He wanted them to win big, really big. "I told the guys today that we should win by 25 or more points if we played up to our potential," Weber said. "I'm trying to find things to challenge them with."

In customary fashion, the Illini rose to their latest challenge. They came out looking like they wanted to win by 50 points, not 25. Brown set the pace by nailing a three-pointer in the first minute, followed by a Williams jump shot, a Head three-pointer and a Powell layup. Just like that, the Illini had a 10-5 lead.

Illinois met Weber's 25-point goal by halftime—it was leading 49-23—and then really turned it on. Early in the second half, the Illini went on a 20-5 roll to extend their lead to 74-35. The crowd at Assembly Hall went nuts during the onslaught, knowing it was watching a team that was at the very top of its game.

The players, on the other hand, were much more low-key. That was their style, in both big games and little ones. "We just played Illinois basketball," Brown said of the dismantling of Valparaiso. "We weren't too excited. We just did our job, got the win."

Actually, they did more than get the win. They reached a new milestone with this one, scoring a season-high 93 points. In addition, each starter reached double figures in scoring for the second straight game, with Brown's 19 points leading the way.

All the while, though, Weber continued to look for new and interesting challenges. His next one was kind of ridiculous—considering the Illini had yet to trail in the second half of a game—but he issued it anyway after the win over the Crusaders: "We've challenged them to win both halves," he said. "We haven't done a great job of taking care of the ball in the second half, and we've talked a lot about winning the second half."

What next? Winning every second of every game?

DECEMBER 22:
ILLINOIS 70, MISSOURI 64

Did it really matter that Missouri was unranked with a pedestrian 6-4 record? Not in the least. These two teams despised each other, so anything was possible each time they met. The animosity between them was such that their annual grudge match had a name: the Braggin' Rights game. Since the contest always took place at a neutral site, the Illini and the Tigers headed to St. Louis and prepared to do battle.

The battle was won by the Illini in the first half...and handily. They did their usual thing, meaning they opened a double-digit lead by halftime, 38-23. But the battle for braggin' rights had only just begun.

Maybe Weber had jinxed Illinois after the Valparaiso game by saying he'd like to see his team play better second-half basketball. Or maybe Missouri simply was playing its best basketball of the year. Whatever the reason, the Fighting Illini just didn't look like the Fighting Illini when the second half began. Their smart and savvy brand of basketball? It was nowhere to be found, as they were beset by foul trouble. Their pinpoint shooting? That, too, disappeared, as swishes were replaced by bricks.

And that opened the door for an epic Missouri comeback. With a minute to go, Illinois' lead had been cut to 65-59—it was a two-possession game. "They raised their level," Weber said of Missouri. "They battled, they fought."

But despite its fast and furious rally, Missouri ran out of time. The Tigers had to start fouling Illinois, and Powell, Head and Williams all hit clutch free throws down the stretch to secure the wobbly victory.

The Illini's streak of dominance ended here, as this was the first game of the season they didn't win by double digits. But a win was a win. Besides, the only streaks that truly mattered were intact: The team still was undefeated and, most importantly, still was No. 1.

The Illini actually were glad Missouri had pushed them to the limit. Now they knew they could win the close ones as well as the blowouts, and this valuable piece of information would serve them well in the coming weeks.

"I'd love to win very game by 20, but that's hard," said Williams, who had 19 points and five assists. "We needed to win a game like this."

DECEMBER 27:
ILLINOIS 105, LONGWOOD 79

The Missouri game had taken a lot out of Illinois, so Longwood showed up on the schedule at the perfect time. This team was the patsy of all patsies. Not only was it playing a full season of Division I ball for the first time, but it also had a 1-13 record. The game would be a laugher.

Or so it seemed.

A funny thing happened to the Illini on the way to their easy victory: They wound up sweating bullets—for a while, anyway. Nothing in the first half signaled what was to come. The Illini coasted to a 56-43 lead behind their typical formula of slick passing and three-point shots. But in a stunning turn of events in the second half, the Lancers rose up and looked capable of pulling off the mother of all upsets. They rallied with a vengeance in the first seven and a half minutes and cut Illinois' lead to a frightful seven points, 63-56.

Said Williams, "We knew we weren't playing with any energy—not playing hard—and they were just getting too many easy baskets."

With around nine minutes to go, however, the Illini's energy level rose to its customary level, and they finally put Longwood back in its place. Late in the game, Illinois even held the Lancers scoreless for nearly four minutes.

But for a program of the Illini's stature, that was of little consolation. Longwood's 79 points were the most any team had scored against Illinois in 2004-05—more than Gonzaga, more than Wake Forest and more than pesky Missouri.

"We've got to click it defensively," said Weber. "That's what made us No. 1. If we don't click it defensively, we're not going to be No. 1 for very long."

At least Illinois' offense wasn't MIA. In fact, the team's 105 points were a season-high. Four of the starters scored in double digits, led by Williams, who had a season-best 23 points. The Illini also received some outstanding work

from the bench; Smith, Ingram and sophomore guard Rich McBride combined for 25 points.

Still, the Lancers—not the Illini—were the ones smiling afterward in the locker room. Said Longwood coach Mike Gillian, "This is extremely significant for our players, for our university."

Illinois, meanwhile, nearly saw its dream season slip away.

DECEMBER 30:
ILLINOIS 69, NORTHWESTERN STATE 51

The Illini literally put as much distance as they could between themselves and the Longwood game. They now were in Sin City competing as the top seed in the Las Vegas Holiday Classic.

The change of scenery agreed with the Illini, although it took them several minutes to regain their normal rhythm. Like Longwood, Northwestern State was intoxicated with the idea of scoring a major upset over the Illini; the Demons tied the score three times in the first half.

But then Northwestern State buckled under the pressure of trying to keep pace with the No. 1 team in the nation. After finally breaking loose and taking a 42-28 lead at the half, Illinois wiped the Demons off the map. Actually, the Demons wiped themselves off the map. Twenty of their 21 total turnovers led to points for Illinois.

As evidenced by Northwestern State's 35.8 shooting percentage from the field, Illinois' defense was back in prime form. And that was fine with Weber, especially considering the debacle against Longwood.

"They wore down," the coach said, "and we wore them down, and they never got going."

After giving up a season-high 79 points to Longwood, the Illini had charged right back and allowed a season-low 51 to Northwestern State. Among the defensive highlights were seven blocked shots, including three from Ingram in only 13 minutes and two from Augustine. Then there was Brown, who was a constant source of irritation to the Demons. The do-it-all guard accounted for four of the Illini's nine steals.

The Illini's offense, on the other hand, struggled, compiling a 41.3 shooting percentage from the field. But the team got a big boost from Head, who scored 18 points and had five three-pointers in nine attempts. Augustine also had an excellent game with 13 points, six of which came

at the foul line.

The Illini now were 13-0, their best start since the 1988-89 season when they reached 17-0 and wound up in the Final Four.

DECEMBER 31:
ILLINOIS 67, CINCINNATI 45

The end of December looked a lot like the beginning of December—with a game against an elite team. And a victory against an elite team. A resounding victory.

The Illini hadn't taken on a ranked contender since their drubbing of then-No. 1 Wake Forest on December 1. The win over the Bearcats, who entered the contest undefeated at 11-0 and were No. 22 in the AP poll, brought perfect closure to the month.

As with the game against Northwestern State, this one was part of the Las Vegas Holiday Classic. But the Illini felt right at home in the desert. There were more than 1,500 Illinois fans in attendance, cheering with the lung capacity of 5,000 fans. They wanted to give Illinois as much help as possible. After all, the Bearcats were a perennial basketball power, and the last time they had played a No. 1 team—Duke in 1998 in the Great Alaska Shootout—they had won.

But there was no chance of a similar scenario unfolding here. Powered by a defense that was brilliant, the Illini took a 17-8 lead within the first eight minutes. By halftime the game was basically over—and not simply because the Illini had their customary double-digit lead, 35-24. Cincinnati was drained. It had nothing left to bring back onto the court.

"Our kids said that the Cincinnati players were complaining that we were too physical," Weber said. "I think that's good. "It shows we can play different styles. We defended so well."

Confounded by the defensive sets Illinois was throwing at them, the Bearcats had an uncharacteristically pathetic shooting percentage of 28.0. And even though Illinois' physical style of basketball enabled the Bearcats to go to the foul line 26 times, they couldn't do much from there either, sinking only 13 of their attempts.

The Illini needed all the defense they could muster since their offense was in a funk with a 39.3 shooting percentage from the field. Said Weber, "They never let us get in a rhythm, and we didn't let them get in a rhythm either."

Whether the offense or defense was leading the way, the Illini were on a tear. They hadn't so much as trailed in a game since December 9 against Georgetown, and they had played from behind in only 21:32 of the season's 560 total minutes. If this continued, Illinois would shatter every record in its book.

JANUARY 5:
ILLINOIS 84, OHIO STATE 65

The most perilous stretch of the schedule was upon Illinois. The Big Ten season was about to begin.

There was no such thing as an upset in the Big Ten. The competition was so fierce that any team could beat any other team on any given day. And Ohio State was just any other team. At 11-2, the Buckeyes had the potential to create all sorts of problems for the Illini.

Historically, at least, the Illini had Ohio State's number. In 158 games against the Buckeyes, the Illini had won 99 times. The record was even better in Champaign, where this game would be played: 57-21.

But this was a new season, and things didn't look particularly rosy for the Illini early on in this matchup. Within the first five minutes of the game, Ohio State took an eight-point lead, 14-6. Making matters worse, Augustine had to leave the floor after his foot was stepped on.

Would Augustine and, in turn, his team go down for the count? Heck, no. "It's the first game of the Big Ten season," he said. "You can't just go out there and quit."

Augustine returned to the floor and promptly led an Illini rally. His layup at 3:27 in the first half tied the score at 33-33. About a minute later, the Illini took the lead, 34-33, on a free throw from Ingram and never again trailed. The game morphed into a typical Illini blowout in the second half, as they outscored Ohio State 38-25.

Illinois found its inspiration from Augustine, who had perhaps the best game of his college career despite his sore foot. Not only did the junior tie his career-high with 21 points, he had 10 rebounds and was 5 of 6 from the foul line.

"Finally, he got some confidence and wants to shoot the ball," Williams said of Augustine. "We just need him to keep doing that. We need him to play like that every game."

Williams himself never lacked confidence when it came to shooting the ball—and this game was no different. He

took a team-high 16 shots, resulting in 14 points. But Williams couldn't be accused of being a selfish player, as evidenced by his eight assists.

Ultimately, though, the game was won in the trenches, where the Illini had 13 offensive rebounds. All told, they outrebounded Ohio State 37-22. The Illini could expect more of the same type of grueling basketball from now on. This was Big Ten basketball, where the toughest team prevailed. In this case, anyway, that team was Illinois, led by its gutsy center.

JANUARY 8:
ILLINOIS 68, PURDUE 59

This was the final season for Purdue coach Gene Keady. The man was a legend, but perhaps he had decided to stick around for one year to long. His players weren't exactly sending him into the sunset in grand style. At 4-7, the Boilermakers were among the Big Ten's worst teams.

But remember, in the Big Ten even the worst teams could rise up and bite the best ones. That was exactly what happened here. Purdue played with more pride and vigor than it had all season, jumping out to a 27-19 lead in the first 10 minutes. The Illini didn't know how to respond. They couldn't pass well or hit three-pointers—two of the staples of their game. By halftime, the Illini were down 39-33. It was the first time in 2004-05 they had been losing at the half. Said Weber, "We knew Purdue would raise their level of play."

Purdue's level of play rose in particular against Brown, who was MIA. The playmaking guard was taken completely out of the mix, not attempting a single shot.

"I had no points, no shots—then I started hitting them," Brown said. "In the second half, they started to play me a little softer, and I shot the ball."

He did indeed. Brown's first points of the day came at the 16:31 mark in the second half, a three-pointer that tied the score at 41-41. Midway through the half, Brown blew the game wide open, nailing two three-pointers in a span of 25 seconds to give the Illini a 56-45 advantage. And when Purdue scratched its way back and narrowed the lead to 56-48, Brown simply hit another three-point shot.

"I told him to play like you're No. 1," Weber said of Brown, who finished the game with 14 points. "I said, 'Somebody has to step up and make plays.'"

Brown's teammates stepped up, too. Augustine had

eight points and nine rebounds, Powell had 13 points and five rebounds, and Head had 15 points and four rebounds. The Illini also took pretty good care of the basketball, turning it over seven times to Purdue's 13. And as was the case against Ohio State, they won the all-important battle of the boards 30-25.

The hard-fought victory moved Illinois to 16-0 and ever closer to history. Only the 1988-89 and 1914-15 teams had started this well. The 1914-15 team went on to win the national championship, and this current edition was starting to conjure the same type of magic.

JANUARY 12:
ILLINOIS 90, PENN STATE 64

Penn State may not have had much of a record (6-9 overall, 0-2 in the Big Ten), but at least it had a plan. To neutralize the Illini's explosive offense, the Nittany Lions set up in a zone defense. Well, you know what they say about the best-laid plans. This one resulted in more history for the Illini, as they sank a best-ever 15 three-pointers in front of the Assembly Hall faithful.

"When teams play zone, there are always open shots for me, Dee and Deron," said Head, who accounted for five of the three-pointers and had 19 points. "We just like to step up and try to show these teams that were good shooters."

Illinois showed Penn State exactly that. After the Nittany Lions took a 10-8 lead within the first five minutes of the game, the three-point barrage started, fueled by Brown, Williams and Head. The Illini went on a soul-crushing 16-0 run and finished off the Nittany Lions by halftime with a 41-25 lead. "It's definitely one of our strengths and a positive weapon," Weber said of his team's ability to shoot the three.

All of those great looks at the basket wouldn't have come, however, without similarly great ball movement. Few teams passed the ball better than the Illini, and this game offered a prime example of that; Illinois had assists on 26 of its 34 baskets. Williams, in particular, did a masterful job of setting up his teammates, registering a team-high and career-high 12 assists. The team's work under the boards also helped bolster its points total; 15 of its 31 rebounds were of the offensive variety.

As had been the case throughout 2004-05, the defense set things up for the offense. The Illini forced 16 turnovers and had nine steals. Smith came off the bench to provide

a huge defensive lift in 15 minutes of play; in addition to a blocked shot, he had two steals.

All of those numbers were impressive, but none more so than this one: January 12 marked the 100th anniversary of Illinois men's basketball. To mark the occasion, the team notched its 1,500th all-time victory. The Illini now were only the 15th NCAA program with 1,500 wins, joining such storied schools as Kentucky, North Carolina, Duke, UCLA and Indiana. The Illini's 1,500th win wasn't quite as dominant as the first one—a 71-4 pounding of Champaign High School—but it was every bit as sweet.

JANUARY 15:
ILLINOIS 78, NORTHWESTERN 66

This game wasn't remarkable in itself, but the ramifications certainly were. In fact, it was a victory no one associated with the program would soon forget. By foiling Northwestern, Illinois ran its record to 18-0, the best start ever for the school.

"We love it," Head said of the mark. "We've done something no one else has done."

Still, the win didn't come as easily as it probably should have. If not for the play of Head, the Illini may not have even gotten it. At the very least, the road would have been a lot rockier. The guard had a season-high 26 points, including four three-pointers.

Illinois needed every point it could get, too. The 7-8 Wildcats weren't an elite Big Ten team, but they had put forth a few excellent efforts in 2004-05. What's more, they had scored an upset win over the Illini in 2003-04, so they couldn't be taken lightly. Throughout this game, Northwestern once again proved to be a worthy adversary. Every time the Illini seemed poised to pull away, the Wildcats would charge back to within striking distance. Early in the first half, they reduced a 10-4 Illinois lead to 10-8; later they fought back from 30-22 to make it 30-26.

The second half brought more of the same. In the opening minutes, Northwestern closed to within four points, 43-39. But then the Illini finally pulled away—led, of course, by Head, who had 17 points in the second half. Said Weber, "Luther had a special day."

Powell also fared well, with 15 points and seven rebounds, including a team-best five on the offensive boards. Smith, meanwhile, provided another stellar effort off the bench, notching eight points, a couple rebounds and a blocked shot.

Given the way Northwestern had played them in 2003-04, the Illini were just happy to escape with a victory. "They're tough to play here [at Welsh-Ryan Arena]," Weber said. "It's tough for anybody to win on the road. So it's rewarding."

The rewards seemed endless in this dream season. After all, each time they added to their winning streak from here on, the Illini would be making even more history.

JANUARY 20:
ILLINOIS 73, IOWA 68 (OT)

History hung in the balance here. So did the No. 1 ranking. If the Missouri game had been a little bit frightening, this one was right out of a Wes Craven movie. The thousands of fans at Assembly Hall were downright terrified by what they saw.

The Illini knew full well that it would be a tough day. Iowa was ranked 23rd in the nation, but more importantly, it was a bitter Big Ten rival. Still, given the way the game began, it seemed as if Illinois would be up to the challenge. Although the Illini had difficulty shooting, they played outstanding defense and took a 34-25 lead into the locker room at halftime.

Then "The Nightmare at Assembly Hall" began. After Brown opened the second half with a three-pointer that extended the Illini's lead to 37-25, the momentum slowly shifted. Illinois missed countless shots, allowing the Hawkeyes to stay within striking distance. Iowa's Jeff Horner made a three-pointer about seven minutes into the half, and teammate Pierre Pierce quickly followed with one of his own. Suddenly, the Illinois lead was a mere three points, 47-44.

The Illini continued to throw up bricks, so Iowa hung around. With 10 seconds remaining and Illinois clinging to a precarious 65-63 lead, the Hawkeyes made their move. Iowa's Greg Brunner rolled in for a layup that tied the game. The 16,618 fans at Assembly Hall gulped collectively. It was onto uncharted territory for this season's Illini: overtime.

When the bonus period began, however, Head rode to the rescue. He had four of their eight overtime points, including a two-point jump shot with 40 seconds remaining that finally broke the back of Iowa. It was the second straight game Head had played the role of the hero.

Despite shooting a season-worst 32.8 percent from the field, turning the ball over 18 times and having only two players score in double digits (Head with 25 and Brown with 12), the Illini somehow had prevailed. The Hawkeyes, meanwhile, were kicking themselves for missing out on a golden opportunity. If they had executed from the foul line, where they were a wretched 6-for12, they could have pulled off the upset.

The way Weber had it figured, a game like this could only help his team. "Maybe we needed a game like this to get a little jolt of energy," Weber said. The Illini needed all the energy they could get because an even bigger test awaited.

JANUARY 25:
ILLINOIS 75, WISCONSIN 65

This game had been circled on everyone's calendar in thick red ink. It was a clash of titans, perfection vs. perfection.

The Badgers, ranked 18th in the nation, hadn't lost at the Kohl Center since Wake Forest beat them on December 4, 2002. Their winning streak at home stood at 38 games, the longest in the nation. Then there was Illinois, which was 19-0.

Someone had to lose.

A strange vibe surrounded the Illini as they prepared for battle. Although they were the country's top team, they felt a lot like an underdog. It was a role they knew well against Wisconsin. Their frustrations in Madison predated the Badgers' current winning streak; Illinois hadn't won a game there since 1998.

As expected, it was a seesaw battle from the opening tip. Illinois took an 11-6 lead within the first five minutes, but Sharif Chambliss and Ray Nixon promptly hit three-pointers to put Wisconsin up 12-11. Then in a dizzying array of shots, Powell hit a three-pointer, Nixon responded with a three, and Brown came back with one of his own. It went on like this throughout the first 20 minutes, and the Illini were clinging to a perilous 35-33 lead at the half.

After the two teams returned to the floor, the streak—the Illini's streak, that is—looked as if it might end. When Wisconsin's Alando Tucker sank a three-point shot at the 12:48 mark, Illinois fell behind 56-48. Time was running out, and, worse, Wisconsin had gained all the momentum.

Despite the dire circumstances, the Illini had one thing in their favor: heart. They simply weren't going to allow themselves to lose. Period. "We picked it up defensively," Weber said. "I'm not sure if they got a little stagnant or tight as it got down the stretch, or if we just defended well."

Whatever the reason, the Illini proceeded to stun the 17,142 people at the Kohl Center, who had known nothing but winning for more than three years. In a span of five minutes, Illinois turned its eight-point deficit into a three-point advantage. Although Wisconsin rallied briefly and reclaimed the lead, 64-61, at the 4:37 mark, Illinois went back on top, 65-64, on a free throw from Ingram with 3:40 remaining. After that, the visitors pulled away.

The Illini had passed their biggest test of the season with flying colors. Said Williams, who finished the night with 13 points, six assists and six rebounds: "We've had a lot of good wins—Wake Forest, Gonzaga. But with this streak that they had here and the history of the building, this is tops right now."

JANUARY 29:
ILLINOIS 89, MINNESOTA 66

The big question was, would the Illini be able to get up for this matchup against Minnesota following their monumental performance at the Kohl Center? The answer came even before the game began. This was the day the school had chosen to officially celebrate the 100-year anniversary of Illini men's basketball, and the joint was rockin'.

Assembly Hall was filled to the gills with dignitaries, including around 300 former players and former coaches Harv Schmidt, Gene Bartow and Lou Henson. Henson received the most rousing ovation of the bunch, and here's why: He was the coach who led the Illini to the Final Four in 1988-89, the last time an Illinois team made it that far.

The 2004-05 squad looked a lot like that high-flyn' group, and not simply because it was wearing replica jerseys from 1988-89. Said Williams, "I think we wanted to come out and put on a show."

Even though Minnesota entered the game with an outstanding 14-5 record, it didn't have as much as a prayer on this day. The Golden Gophers were spooked by the festive atmosphere in Assembly Hall, turning the ball over on each of their first two possessions to set the tone. Thanks to three-pointers from Head and Powell, the Illini mounted a 10-1 lead within the first three minutes. At halftime, that lead was an insurmountable 21 points, 47-26. Illinois

also cruised through the next half, at one time extending the margin to 26 points.

The entire Illini team got into the action. Four starters reached double figures in scoring, paced by Powell, who had 21 points and was 8 of 12 from the field. Williams, meanwhile, put on the show he had promised, totaling 18 points, six assists, five rebounds and two steals.

The Illini overwhelmed Minnesota in nearly conceivable way. They outrebounded the Gophers, 35-30; outshot them from three-point range, 45.5 to 28.6 percent; outshot them from the free-throw line, 76.5 to 73.7 percent; and outshot them overall from the field, 55.9-38.1 percent.

The 100-year celebration had gone off without a hitch, much like the entire season. And as those dignitaries left Assembly Hall, they had a sense that the fun was just beginning for the 2004-05 team.

FEBRUARY 1:
ILLINOIS 81, MICHIGAN STATE 68

What a difference a couple days could make. When the Illini arrived in East Lansing, Mich., they weren't greeted with handshakes and pats on the back from their school's most legendary basketball figures. No, this was enemy territory.

Michigan State had some of the most rabid fans in college basketball. They expected nothing less than the best from their Spartans, and they often were richly rewarded. Michigan State was a perennial national power. This season, it was the highest-ranked Big Ten team Illinois would face, perched at No. 12 in the AP poll.

But those rabid Michigan State fans weren't able to give their team much of a boost on this day. In fact, the results for Illinois were about the same as they had been against Minnesota. Although the Spartans kept the game close early in the first half, the Illini pulled away when they unleashed a torrent of three-pointers. A 12-9 Illinois deficit turned into a 41-33 halftime lead on eight three-point conversions, including a trio from Brown.

Why was Brown so hyped up on this day? He wanted to stick it to those Michigan State fans. "In the warm-ups, I shot two air balls, and the fans started talking trash," Brown said. "When people start talking trash, it just puts fuel in my tank. I knew I was going to get hot."

Brown, along with his teammates, stayed hot in the sec-

ond half. The Illini buried four more three-pointers and, in the process, also buried Michigan State. All told, Illinois was 13 of 24 from three-point range, with five different players contributing at least one trey.

The Illini's outstanding perimeter shooting compensated for problems in other aspects of their game. The Spartans had twice as many offensive rebounds as Illinois did (10-5), but they weren't able to do anything with those extra scoring opportunities. Ultimately, they were done in by a mediocre shooting percentage of 42.9 from the field.

Now the Big Ten title was there for the taking for Illinois. With eight games left, the Illini were two games ahead of both the Spartans and the Badgers in the standings. But the Fighting Illini were chasing something even bigger than that. At 22-0, they were tied with the 1961-62 Buckeyes for the fourth-best start to a season in Big Ten history. The record was held by the 1975-76 Indiana squad, which went 32-0.

FEBRUARY 6:
ILLINOIS 60, INDIANA 47

As fate would have it, Indiana was next up for Illinois. But these Hoosiers were a long, long way from the team of 1975-76, both in years and ability. There was nothing historic about this bunch. An undefeated season? That dream had died long ago. At 10-9, the Hoosiers simply were trying to stay above .500—and even that modest goal was in jeopardy.

Illinois began with a 10-1 run—with eight of those points coming from Augustine—and then extended its lead to 20-3 with 8:39 remaining in the half. It was as dominant a stretch as the Illini had put together all season.

But maybe the Hoosiers had visions of 1975-76 dancing in their heads. Suddenly, their defense clamped down while their offense starting making clutch shots. Illinois, meanwhile, was mired in foul trouble. In the final eight and a half minutes of the half, the Hoosiers outscored Indiana 17-6, narrowing their deficit to six points, 26-20.

But in the end, reality slapped the Hoosiers in the face. This wasn't 1975-76. It was 2004-05, and the Illini were the ones aiming at perfection. They resolved their first-half issues and did just enough to grow the margin of victory to 13 points. Brown, in particular, helped reinvigorated the Illini early in the final half. He hit two three-pointers in less than a minute to put the game away.

Still, this wasn't a pretty victory. The Illini's 60 points were the fewest they had scored in 2004-05. It was a particularly tough game for Williams, who was 0-for-7 from the field but did manage 11 assists. The team as a whole shot only 43.2 percent from the field, although it was saved by its stellar work from the free-throw line, where it was 18 of 20 (90 percent). Head was 6 of 7 from the foul line, with many of those conversions coming down the stretch in the second half.

Weber, of course, was concerned by what he had seen. "We weren't sharp, that's for sure," said the coach. "You're not going to play perfect all the time. You wish you could, but we didn't."

At least the Illini were 23-0. That was as perfect as they needed to be.

FEBRUARY 8:
ILLINOIS 57, MICHIGAN 51

Michigan, like the Hoosiers, had it a rough patch. The Wolverines were mired in their longest losing streak since 1999-2000 (six games) and had dropped their past three by an average of 24 points.

It should have been a cakewalk for the Illini, but it wasn't.

Illinois started strong, mounting a 23-15 lead in the first 11 minutes behind four three-point conversions. But then the Illini went cold, colder than they had gone the entire season. They didn't sink another field goal the rest of the half—their lone point came on a free throw from Powell—and went into the locker room trailing 28-24. It was only the second time all season the Illini had been behind at the half.

The halftime break didn't help much. When the Illini took the floor again, they still were unable to regain their Midas touch. Three more agonizing minutes elapsed before Illinois finally converted a field goal, a layup by Augustine. Amazingly, the Illini were behind only 30-26 after Augustine scored, but they couldn't capitalize on their good fortune. They went cold again, and Michigan stretched its lead to 34-26.

The Illini needed someone to step up in a hurry, and Brown did just that with 13:36 remaining. Brown buried a three-point shot to close the gap to 34-29. Then he made a layup at the 7:54 mark to tie the score at 41-41, followed by a free throw that broke the deadlock. After that, the Illini were able to grind out the victory. But considering the quality of the competition, the game was a lot closer than it should have been.

"We've won a couple this year ugly," said Brown, who also had four steals, three of which of came during the Illini's pivotal rally in the second half. "You can't beat everyone by 20 or 15."

Was the pressure of trying to remain undefeated finally starting to get to the Illini, who once had seemed so unflappable? A little bit. Said Brown, who had a team-high 16 points in the win over Michigan: "There's a bigger target on us now."

The pressure already had gotten the better of the nation's other undefeated team, Boston College. The same day the Illini survived its scare from Michigan, Boston College was upset by Notre Dame. Only one perfect team remained: Illinois.

FEBRUARY 12:
ILLINOIS 70, WISCONSIN 59

It had been a grueling journey for the Illini, but they could see the light at the end of the tunnel. Wisconsin was the last real obstacle Illinois would face in the regular season.

This matchup seemed as if it would be easier than the last one, as the Badgers wouldn't benefit from their imposing home-court advantage. They had to travel to Assembly Hall, where a record 16,865 fans were waiting for them. Nevertheless, as evidenced by their No. 20 ranking in the AP poll, the Badgers were fighters. They had proved that against the Illini earlier in the season.

And they proved it again, mostly because the Illini's shooting woes from the Michigan game carried over into this one. Illinois had plenty of good looks at the basket early on, but it couldn't do anything with them. Making matters worse, both Brown and Powell got into foul trouble and had to spend large portions of the first half on the bench. As a result of the fouls and the poor shooting, the Illini led by the slimmest of margins at the half, 27-26. If Wisconsin had been able to do anything from the foul line, where it was just 2 of 8, it would have been winning.

Early in the second half, however, the Illini got into a groove. Sparked by eight points from Williams, they went on a 10-0 run that made the score 37-28. But Wisconsin hung tough, narrowing the Fighting Illini lead to 54-49 with four minutes remaining.

Illinois needed a hero again—it needed Brown. He showed up right on time, sinking two three-pointers and two free throws in the final three minutes to ice the game. Afterward, Brown was quick to spread the credit to his teammates, saying "These guys got me the ball in good position."

And even though Brown was the one who made the highlight-reel shots, it was Head who did the heavy lifting. He led the team in both points (26) and rebounds (8), and was 12 of 13 from the foul line.

The Illini made yet more history with his nail-biting victory. It was their 25th consecutive win, a new school record. The old one—and we mean old—had been set about nine decades earlier, when the Illini rattled off 25 consecutive victories from February 1914 to February 1916.

FEBRUARY 16:
ILLINOIS 83, PENN STATE 63

How many more ways could the Fighting Illini find to be perfect? Powell discovered a new one against Penn State, going 10-for-10 from he field.

"It was good to make some baskets," said the ever-modest Powell, who finished the game with 21 points, "but the guards set me up."

There never was any doubt about which team would win this game. The Illini shot out to a 7-0 lead on baskets from Augustine and Powell and then a three-pointer from Brown. Penn State rallied briefly, closing to within two points at 9-7, but then the fun began in earnest. Illinois hit shots from anywhere and everywhere, and built up a laughable 52-30 lead at halftime.

The Illini had grown used to their status as the No. 1 team in the nation, and now they could enjoy it. "There's not much stress here," Weber said. "You might think it's a loony bin and not a stressful team." Indeed, the Nittany Lions were the ones feeling all the stress. "I think we broke their spirit down the stretch in the first half," the coach added.

For good measure, the Illini stomped on Penn State's broken spirit a few times in the second half. At the 10:43 mark, they stretched their lead to 30 points (74-44) before easing up on their overmatched opponent and sending in the reserves.

The Illini outclassed the Nittany Lions in every phase of the game. They shot more accurately (54-44%), gobbled up more total rebounds (30-24) and offensive rebounds (9-7), blocked more shots (4-1), had more steals (11-3) and turned the ball over fewer times (8-15).

The individual stats were just as impressive. Every starter except Williams scored in double digits, though he still contributed to the cause by racking up 11 assists. Brown had the most complete game, tallying 19 points, 11 assists, four rebounds, and two steals. Ingram, meanwhile, was the best of the bench players with five points and four rebounds, including two on the offensive boards.

This was exactly the type of victory the Illini needed as March Madness approached—they were peaking at the perfect time. "Streaks aren't important," Weber said of his team's perfect season. "Winning the Big Ten, getting the high seed, and advancing March into April is what's important."

FEBRUARY 19:
ILLINOIS 75, IOWA 65

The Illini had ample reason to worry heading into this showdown. Iowa, remember, had taken Illinois into overtime back in January, nearly ruining its perfect season. And even though the Hawkeyes now were without their best player—guard Pierre Pierce, who had been kicked off the team—they never had any difficulties getting up for this rivalry.

Once again, Iowa kept the Illini on their heels. It went up 13-12 at the 11:25 mark in the first half and 18-17 with 8:06 remaining. Then after Illinois had regained the lead again, the Hawkeyes charged back and tied the score at 20-20 on a dunk by Erek Hansen with 5:28 to go. Fouls and poor shooting were the main problems for the Illini, although they did manage to give themselves some breathing room—a 36-28 lead—by he half.

"We're going to keep coming at teams," Brown said. "If our shots aren't falling, we're going to keep shooting and making plays."

The Illini came out swinging in the second half. Williams hit two jump shots in the opening minute to extend the Illinois lead to 40-28 and put even more pressure on the Hawkeyes. Although Iowa made one last valiant comeback—closing to 60-58 late in the game—Brown helped his team pull away by rattling off seven points. Without Pierce, the Hawkeyes lacked depth and ultimately ran out of steam.

All told, it was a huge day for Brown, who tied Williams with a team-high 18 points and also was 3-for-4 from the free-throw line.

"Stuff like this happens all year," Williams said of Brown. "It seems like every game, somebody steps up and does something at the right time."

Against Iowa, Williams himself was one of those players. In addition to his 18 points, he had five assists and a team-best three steals.

The real key to the victory, however, was the Illini's ball-handling. They turned the ball over just nine times, whereas Iowa shot itself in the foot with 21 turnovers.

Illinois was closing in fast on the Big Ten title. If it won its following two games—against Northwestern and Purdue at home—the championship banner would fly at Assembly Hall. And if the Illini won their season-finale at Ohio State on March 6, it would become the first team since Indiana in 1975-76 to go undefeated in the Big Ten.

"If we take care of business at home, now we can clinch the outright title, then go see what happens at Ohio State," Weber said. "But that's a long way off. Right now, we're worried about the bus ride home and Northwestern."

FEBRUARY 23:
ILLINOIS 84, NORTHWESTERN 48

As it turned out, Weber needn't have worried about either the bus ride or Northwestern. The Illini got home just fine, and then they proceeded to obliterate the Wildcats.

Brown set the pace, nailing four four-pointers in the first 10 minutes. His fourth one gave the Illini a 26-13 lead, and he immediately followed that with a layup.

"I hit my first two [three-point shots], and that confidence just kept building," Brown said. "I felt like I could shoot anywhere."

As if to prove his point, Brown made yet another trey with 33 seconds left in the half to give his team a 45-21 lead. The rout was on. The Illini's first-half stats were out of this world. They shot 60 percent from the floor (18-for-30), the sixth time they had reached that plateau this season in the opening half. Illinois was just as impressive on the defensive side; Northwestern's 22 points were the fewest allowed by the Illini in a first half in 2004-05.

The onslaught didn't slow in the next half. Powell scored six of the Illini's first nine points as they extended their advantage to 54-22. When Warren Carter dunked the ball at the 7:19 mark, the Illinois lead became 41 points, 75-34.

On the night, the Illini hit 59.3 percent of their shots from the floor and had nearly twice as many rebounds as the Wildcats (36-20). Brown, of course, led Illinois in scoring with 20 points, but he was closely followed by Powell's 18. Powell also had a team-high 10 rebounds.

This was the Illini's 24th straight Big Ten win and their 20th straight win at Assembly Hall. In addition, they needed just three more victories to tie the single-season school record. But no one was paying much attention to those milestones. Here's the one that mattered most to everyone involved: The victory over Northwestern clinched at least a tie for the Big Ten title.

"We win two more games, and we go undefeated in the regular season, which only one other team has done in the Big Ten," Weber said. "[And] another outright [Big Ten] title. There are a lot of things on the line."

Whatever happened from here, the 2004-05 Illini had assured themselves of a prominent place in the school's history book.

The Coach

The Coach

Despite what the national media think, Bruce Weber didn't come from nowhere

Geez, nothing like paying your dues.

People may look at University of Illinois men's head basketball coach Bruce Weber and say, "Gee, he sure is a lucky guy."

After all, he walked into a program two years ago after Bill Self left for Kansas University and inherited a talented, ready-for-prime-time bunch that hasn't disappointed in the least – especially this season. And Weber himself wasn't exactly a household name on the major college basketball scene.

He was just plying away at his trade for five seasons (1998-2003) at mid-major Southern Illinois University in Carbondale before hitting the bit-time in Champaign. But how about before that? He put in some 18 years as an assistant to Gene Keady at Purdue University before the Salukis came calling. Eighteen years without getting a head coaching job. How's that for persistence and patience?

"I'm proud of what Bruce has done," Keady said of his former pupil's success at SIU and U of I. "But, unfortunately, we're in the same league. That was dumb of me... Recommending my assistants to be coaches in this league is stupid."

Mediocrity was where the Salukis were mired prior to Weber's arrival in 1998. Three losing seasons preceded Weber, yet he had nary a one in five years. By his second season, the Salukis garnered a berth in the National Invitational Tournament with a 20-13 mark but fell back to 16-14 in 2000-2001.

But that was the calm before the Saluki storm. SIU blitzed the Missouri Valley Conference in '01-02, winning a share of the league crown and reaching the finals of the MVC postseason tourney, which secured an at-large berth in the NCAA tournament. And that wasn't all. Playing in front of a Chicago audience in regional action, the Salukis knocked off Texas Tech and Georgia, before being derailed by Connecticut in the Sweet Sixteen. The 28-8 mark set a school record for wins in a season.

In addition, SIU Arena recorded its first sellout in 12 years that season. Carbondale was abuzz with Saluki basketball, and that was due in no small part to Weber. "He is the best manager of people I've ever been around," said SIU assistant Rodney Watson. "He enjoys basketball and wants everyone in the program to equally enjoy it."

The Salukis enjoyed more riches in what turned out to be Weber's swan song. SIU finished the 2002-03 campaign with a 22-5 record, an MVC regular season championship and another berth in the NCAA tournament. For his efforts, Weber was named the MVC Coach of the Year.

In his first five seasons as a head coach, Weber compiled a 103-54 record, three postseason tournament berths – including two trips to the NCAAs – an MVC regular-season title and a nod as coach of the year. Not bad for a first-timer.

Weber credits his time beside Keady (including the 1979-80 season at Western Kentucky) with pointing him in the right direction. Consistent success will do that for a person. The Boilermakers made the postseason 17 times, won six Big Ten titles, reached the NCAA Sweet Sixteen twice and the Elite Eight once. Weber also assisted the USA Team at the World University Games in 1989 and the Pan American Games in '91.

"One of the best things that ever happened to me was being an assistant for so long because I saw everything," Weber said. "We were No. 2 at Purdue. It helped me understanding what it was like. Then we make the run at SIU. Every experience – if you're smart – you take it all in and you learn from it, and you use it."

"I've said I would only take a job where I felt I had an opportunity to be at a national program at a place where I had a chance to finish my career and have a chance of winning a national championship," he said in accepting the Illinois job. "And I believe this is it."

SIU athletic director Paul Kowalczyk addressed the media acknowledging Weber's impact as the coach was departing for greener pastures in Champaign:

"You know, a few years ago if we'd have a press conference to recognize a change in the Saluki head men's basketball coaching position, the crowd would have been a lot smaller. At the time, we had a basketball team, now we have a basketball program. Bruce worked hard to build the program, and SIU's indebted to him for his service here. "

And to think he was just this close to accepting another head coaching job – in the Big Ten, no less.

There was talk of Weber succeeding Keady in West Lafayette after serving a season as an associate head coach during Keady's farewell season. In fact it was more than just talk.

But somewhere along the line, that scenario didn't happen and Keady is still on the Purdue bench in his final season. "There was no certainty when Gene would depart," Weber said then, and leaving a successful head coaching spot to return to the assistant ranks with no clear time frame of ascending to the head job didn't appeal to Weber.

Ironically enough, former Boilermaker star Matt Painter sits next to Keady now. He replaced Weber at SIU for one year before being offered the same "grooming" spot beside Keady.

The University of Illinois was in need of a head coach following the 2002-03 season after Self. Since the departure of longtime head man Lou Henson, the Illini maintained a winning tradition through the brief tenures of Lon Kruger (81-48 from 1997-2000) and Self (78-24 from 2001-2003), and athletic director Ron Guenther had no attention of letting the program slip into mediocrity.

Weber's winning experiences as both an assistant and head coach had Guenther at Weber's doorstep. It was Weber's time to return to the Big Ten, only this time as the commander of his own ship.

Soon after, Weber inked a five-year deal to become the Illini's 16th head coach, and the deal even included a $1 million buyout clause. Guenther wanted no part of a coach skipping out after a couple years again, hence the hefty buyout.

"I've said I would only take a job where I felt I had an opportunity to be at a national program at a place where I had a chance to finish my career and have a chance of winning a national championship," he said in accepting the job. "And I believe this is it."

The transition wasn't without hurdles, though. Players loyal to Self weren't happy about the change and thought of transferring. Then there's the distrust issue of bringing in a new coach. Weber had to wade through all that in his first campaign with the Blue and Orange, and he even went so far as to hold a mock funeral to put an end to the Self Era and make his own imprint.

Also, there was the grumbling from the players about Weber's motion offense. The team struggled some, yes, but things came together in the second half of the 2003-04 season. The players become more comfortable and began to trust him, and he got to know them as well, on and off the court.

The result? With just one senior on his roster, Weber became just the third coach in the history of the Big Ten to win an outright title in his first year at a school (Guy Lowmann at Wisconsin in 1918 and Bill Musselman at Minnesota in 1972 were the others). The Illini won 26 games – third highest in school history – and reached the Sweet Sixteen for the third time in four seasons.

The expectations were even higher entering this, the 100th season of Illini basketball. And the Illini didn't disappoint. The Illini recorded the best start in team history (16-0 was the old mark) and became just the 15th college basketball program to win 1,500 games. They've spent the majority of the season at the top of the college basketball heap.

"He's our catalyst," said Illini star guard Deron Williams. "I'd be surprised if he wasn't a candidate for national coach of the year this year. I can't say enough about what he's done."

Regardless of how this season plays out, there are questions for the future. Weber largely is getting results from the players Self recruited, not unlike Self benefited from Kruger's personnel. What that does say is these coaches are able to get results from players they didn't actually recruit. So if Weber is in it for the long haul, what kind of recruiter will he be and will he be able to maintain the level of Illini success of his predecessors and what he's already achieved?

If he has his way, Bruce Weber will have plenty of time to write a few more chapters of this Illini tale.

The Players

Luther Head

Born ....Nov. 26, 1982
Class ....Senior
Position ....Guard
Height/weight 6-3, 182
Hometown ....Chicago
Major ....Sports Management

AT ILLINOIS

2003-04 Junior: Ranked fourth on the team and 24th in scoring with 11.0 points per game. Erupted for a career-high 29 points on 9-of-14 shooting with four 3-pointers in Big Ten Tournament quarterfinal victory over Indiana. Averaged 7.0 assists and 5.5 rebounds in Illinois' two NCAA Tournament victories. Third on the team in assists on the season (75). Illini were 21-3 with him in the starting lineup.

2002-03 Sophomore: Pelvic injury slowed him during the season and caused him to miss seven games, but he still started eight games and played more than 20 minutes per contest. Fourth on the team in scoring, averaging 7.9 points. Shot 42.4 percent from 3-point land (28-of-66). Also hit 51.9 percent of his shots from the floor (68-of-131).

2001-02 Freshman: True freshman started 13 games, including 11 of the last 12, and averaged 4.5 points in 16.6 minutes per game for the season. Second on the team with 34 steals. Shot 51 percent from the field (63-of-124).

HIGH SCHOOL

Averaged 22 points, 8 rebounds, 6 assists and 5 steals as a senior in the rugged Red-West Division of the Chicago Public League. Earned First-Team All-State honors in 2001 from the Chicago Tribune, Chicago Sun-Times, Champaign-Urbana News-Gazette, Associated Press and Illinois Basketball Coaches Association. Played in the

Wendy's All-Star Classic. First Illinois recruit out of the Chicago Public League since 1994. Averaged over 20 points, 8 assists and 7 rebounds per game as a junior at Manley Academy.

Deron Williams

Born . . . . .June 26, 1984
Class . . . . .Junior
Position . . . . .Guard
Height/weight .6-3, 210
Hometown . . . . .The Colony, Texas
Major . . . . .Sports management

AT ILLINOIS

2004-05 Junior: Preseason Wooden Award All-America candidate. Playboy preseason All-American. Athlon Sports preseason honorable mention All-American, Big Ten Player of the Year and First-Team All-Big Ten. Lindy's preseason First-Team All-Big Ten. Street & Smith's preseason All-Big Ten.

2003-04 Sophomore: First-Team All-Big Ten selection by coaches and media. Big Ten All-Tournament Team. USBWA All-District 5 selection. Led the Illini and ranked eighth in the Big Ten in scoring, averaging 14.0 points. Just the third player in Big Ten history to lead the league in assists each of his first two seasons in the conference (Magic Johnson, Bruce Douglas). Season average of 6.17 assists ranks third in Illini history. Ranked second in the league with an assist/turnover ratio of 2.47 and sixth in 3-point shooting at 39.4 percent. Also sixth in the Big Ten in 3-pointers per game with 2.23 average.

2002-03 Freshman: True freshman started 30 of 32 games for the Illini at guard. Named All-Freshman Team by CollegeInsider.com. Second on the team and ranked third in the Big Ten in assists, averaging 4.53 per game. Led the league in assists in conference play with 77 (4.81 apg). One of 12 players on the 2002 USA Basketball Men's Junior World Championship Qualifying Team. Helped the U.S. to a bronze medal along with fellow Illini Dee Brown.

HIGH SCHOOL

Consensus Top 50 recruit nationally. Averaged 17.6 points, 8.4 assists, 6.1 rebounds and 2.6 steals per game as a senior. Averaged 17 points, 9.4 assists, five rebounds and two steals per game as a junior.

Daniel "Dee" Brown

Born . . . . .Aug. 17, 1984
Class . . . . .Junior
Position . . . . .Guard
Height/weight .6-0,185
Hometown . . . . .Maywood, Ill.
Major . . . . .Sports management

AT ILLINOIS

2004-05 Junior: Preseason Wooden Award All-America candidate. Athlon Sports preseason honorable mention All-American and First-Team All-Big Ten. Lindy's preseason First-Team All-Big Ten. Street & Smith's preseason All-Big Ten.

2003-04 Sophomore: Second-Team All-Big Ten selection by coaches and media. Honorable mention All-American by Associated Press. Big Ten All-Tournament Team. Academic All-Big Ten selection. Started every game of the season, ranking second on the team and 14th in the Big Ten in scoring at 13.3 points per game. Led the Illini in steals with 51. Ranked second on the team and in the Big Ten with 4.5 assists per game. Fourth on the team in rebounding at 3.7 per game.

2002-03 Freshman: Second-Team All-Big Ten selection by the media and Third-Team All-Big Ten by league coaches. Named to first-ever Big Ten All-Freshman Team. Named All-Freshman Team by CollegeInsider.com. Started 31-of-32 games at guard, leading the team in minutes played at 34.1 mpg. Second on the team in scoring, averaging 12.0 points. Big Ten leader in assist-to-turnover ratio in all games (+2.56) and conference games (+3.04) . One of 12 players on the 2002 USA Basketball Men's Junior World Championship Qualifying Team. Helped the U.S. to a bronze medal along with fellow Illini Deron Williams.

HIGH SCHOOL

Earned Mr. Basketball honors in Illinois following his senior season. The ninth Mr. Basketball to attend Illinois since the award began in 1981. Named Illinois' Gatorade Player of the Year in 2002. McDonald's All-American. Champaign-Urbana News-Gazette Illinois Player of the Year in 2002. First-Team All-State pick by the IBCA, Chicago Tribune, Chicago Sun-Times, Champaign-Urbana News-Gazette. Finished his high school career as Proviso East's all-time leader in scoring, assists and steals. Averaged 25.6 points, 5.5 assists and 2.9 steals per game as a senior.

James Augustine

Born . . . . .Feb. 27, 1984
Class . . . . .Junior
Position . . . . .Forward
Height/weight .6-10, 230
Hometown . . . . .Mokena, Ill.
Major . . . . .Sports management

AT ILLINOIS

2003-04 Sophomore: Honorable mention All-Big Ten selection started every game of the season. Academic All-Big Ten selection. Led Illini in rebounding with a 7.3 average, ranking fourth in the Big Ten. Second in the Big Ten in field goal percentage at .635 (125-197). Fifth in the Big Ten in blocked shots at 1.3 per game. Led the Illini with seven double-doubles during the season. Scored at least nine points in 21 games. Led team in rebounding 17 times.

2002-03 Freshman: Named to first-ever Big Ten All-Freshman Team. Started 29 of 32 games. Second on the team in field-goal percentage, shooting 58.0 percent (94-162). Ranked third in the Big Ten in field-goal percentage during conference play at 58.6 percent (51-87). Second on the team in rebounding, averaging

HIGH SCHOOL

Earned First-Team All-State honors from the Champaign-Urbana News-Gazette after averaging 18 points, 10.6 rebounds and 4 blocked shots per game. Averaged 14 points, 7 rebounds and 5 blocks as a junior. Consensus Top 100 recruit nationally. Multi-sport athlete also played football (lettered in 2001 at quarterback) and baseball (lettered in 2001 and 2002 as a pitcher) at Lincoln-Way Central.

Uncle Jerry Augustine played professional baseball in the Milwaukee Brewers organization from 1973-85. Uncle

Dick Sorensen played football for the Miami Hurricanes from 1965-70 while cousin Nick Sorensen played football at Virginia Tech from 1995-00 and with the St. Louis Rams.

Roger Powell

Born . . . . .Jan. 15, 1983
Class . . . . .Senior
Position . . . . .Forward
Height/weight 6-6, 235
Hometown . . . . .Joliet, Ill.
Major . . . . .Speech communications

AT ILLINOIS

2003-04 Junior: Honorable mention All-Big Ten selection. Started 31 games of the season. Third on the Illini and 20th in the Big Ten in scoring at 11.6 points per game. Second on the team (20th in Big Ten) in rebounding at 5.0 boards per game. Ranked third in the Big Ten in field goal shooting at 59.5 percent (150-252). Second on the team with 75 offensive rebounds, ranking 10th in the Big Ten in offensive rebounds with 2.34 per game. Scored career-high 24 points and grabbed nine boards at Wisconsin on Jan. 24.

2002-03 Sophomore: Named to the Big Ten All-Tournament Team after leading Illinois with 16 points in the tournament title game vs. Ohio State and scoring 14 vs. Northwestern in the quarterfinals. Started 19 games during the season, including 10 of the last 11. Finished second in the Big Ten in field goal percentage in all games, hitting 59.1 percent from the field (104-176). Led the Big Ten in field goal percentage in conference games, connecting on 64.1 percent of his shots (50-78). Third on the team in scoring, averaging 8.7 points. Scored a season-high 22 points vs. Indiana (2/25) on 9-of-13 shooting.

2001-02 Freshman: True freshman played in 27 games on the year, averaging 2.9 points and 1.8 rebounds per game. Scored season-high 12 points against Western Illinois, hitting four field goals and adding four free throws. Played a season-high 15 minutes against Loyola-Chicago, tallying five points and five rebounds.

HIGH SCHOOL

Earned First-Team All-State honors at Joliet in 2001 from the Chicago Tribune, Chicago Sun-Times, Champaign-Urbana News-Gazette, Associated Press and Illinois Basketball Coaches Association. Also earned First-Team All-State honors in 2000 from the Champaign-Urbana News-Gazette, Chicag Tribune and Chicago Sun-Times. A consensus Top 100 prospect. Fourth in voting for Mr. Basketball in Illinois following his senior season. As a junior, averaged 19 points and 8 rebounds in leading the Steelmen to a 20-8 mark. Shot 58 percent from the field, 71 percent from the line and 38 percent from three-point range as a junior. Second-team All-State by AP and Illinois Basketball Coaches Association as a junior.

Fred Nkemdi

Born	Oct. 28, 1982
Class	Senior
Position	Forward
Height/weight	6-5, 235
Hometown	North Riverside, Ill.
Last College	Morton Junior College
Major	Political Science

AT ILLINOIS

2003-04 Junior: Gained his eligibility prior to the spring 2004 semester after earning a spot on the team during open tryouts in October. Played in six games.

AT MORTON COLLEGE

Averaged 15 points and 10 rebounds per game for the Panthers. Earned All-Skyway Community College Conference honors and was the Morton College Academic Athlete of the Year.

HIGH SCHOOL

Lettered as a junior and senior in basketball at Riverside-Brookfield and as a senior in football. Earned All-Suburban Prairie White Conference honors in basketball as a senior. Finished 13th in the 2000 IHSA Slam Dunk contest.

Warren Carter

Born . . . . .April 23, 1985
Class . . . . .Sophomore
Position . . . . .Forward
Height/weight 6-9, 210
Hometown . . . . .Dallas, Texas
Major . . . . .Liberal Arts & Sciences

AT ILLINOIS

2004-05 Sophomore: Traveled to Europe over the summer with the Big Ten Men's Basketball Foreign Tour Team. Was the team's fifth leading scorer, averaging 9.6 points, and the third leading rebounder, averaging 4.4 rebounds.

2003-04 Freshman: Lanky freshman saw action in 17 games. Scored season-high nine points and grabbed three rebounds in season-opening win over Western Illinois Nov. 22. Scored three points in win over Maryland-Eastern Shore Dec. 11.

HIGH SCHOOL

Texas Class 5A Player of the Year as a senior. Texas Association of Basketball Coaches All-State selection. Dallas Morning News All-Area pick. Played in the THSCA and TABC All-Star games. Dallas area Defensive Player of the Year. Averaged 25.6 points, 12.3 rebounds and 5.2 blocks per game as a senior, making 45 3-pointers (37 percent) and shooting 56 percent from the field and 75 percent from the free-throw line. Totaled 788 points, 77 steals, 371 rebounds and 143 blocks during his senior season. Averaged 23.3 points, 10.7 rebounds and 3.5 blocked shots as a junior. Consensus Top 100 recruit.

Richard McBride

Born . . . . .Jan. 29, 1985
Class . . . . .Sophomore
Position . . . . .Guard
Height/weight .6-3, 215
Hometown . . . . .Springfield, Ill.
Major . . . . .Liberal Arts & Sciences

AT ILLINOIS

2003-04 Freshman: Played in 29 games, averaging over 14 minutes per game. Emerged on the scene with season-high 22 points in 29 minutes of play in win over Memphis Dec. 13. Nailed 6-of-10 3-pointers against Memphis, tying the most 3-pointers in a game by a Big Ten player on the season. Also had season highs of five assists and five rebounds against Memphis. His 24 three-pointers were fourth-most on the team.

HIGH SCHOOL

Three-time All-State selection by the Champaign News-Gazette and Chicago Sun-Times and two-time pick by the Associated Press, Illinois Basketball Coaches Association (IBCA) and Chicago Tribune. Finished third in voting for Illinois' Mr. Basketball as a senior. Four-year letter winner at Lanphier under Craig Patton, helping the Lions to a 104-23 mark. Finished his high school career as Lanphier's all-time leading scorer with 2,068 points. Averaged 24.6 points, 7.9 rebounds and 2.3 assists per game as a senior Made 82 3-pointers as a senior. Earned All-Conference honors all four years of high school. EA Sports All-American. Fourth-Team Parade All-American. Averaged 18 points, 5 rebounds and 4 assists as a junior, while shooting 49 percent from the field and 43 percent from 3-point range. Averaged 17 points as a sophomore, and was the conference player of the year. Averaged 14 points per game as a freshman and finished third in the Central State Eight Player of the Year voting, while being named All-Conference.

Nick Smith

Born . . . . .Sept. 25, 1982
Class . . . . .Redshirt Senior
Position . . . . .Center
Height/weight 7-2, 250
Hometown . . . . .Valrico, Fla.
Major . . . . .Finance

AT ILLINOIS

2003-04 Junior: Academic All-Big Ten selection. Sixth on the team in scoring with 6.8 points and fifth in rebounds with 3.2 boards. One of the top free-throw shooters in the Big Ten, making over 80 percent of his free throws for two consecutive seasons. Scored in double figures in 10 games with a career-high 22 points in win over Ohio State on Jan. 7. Also grabbed a career-high tying nine rebounds against Ohio State

2002-03 Sophomore: Academic All-Big Ten selection. Shot 66.7 percent (34-of-51) from the field over his last 16 games of the season. Made 67.3 percent of his shots (33-of-49) during Big Ten play. Led the Illini in free throw shooting at 86.4 percent (38-of-44).

2001-02 Freshman: Academic All-Big Ten selection. Played in 33 of 35 games starting four times. Averaged 3.8 points on 54 percent shooting from the field (49-of-91). Earned his first career start against Loyola-Chicago, responding with season highs of 17 points and nine rebounds against the Ramblers.

2000-01 Redshirt: Sat out the season as a redshirt. Retained four years of eligibility.

HIGH SCHOOL

Florida Gatorade Player of the Year in 2000. Second-Team All-State selection as a senior after being named

honorable mention All-State as a junior First-Team All-Conference and All-Hillsborough County performer as a senior. Averaged 25 points, 14 rebounds and five blocks as a senior. Averaged 17 points, 15 rebounds and eight blocks as a junior.

Jack Ingram

Born . . . . .April 23, 1982
Class . . . . .Redshirt Senior
Position .Forward/Center
Height/weight .6-10, 245
Hometown . . . . .San Antonio, Texas
Last College . . . . .Tulsa
Major . . . . .Electrical engineering

AT ILLINOIS

2003-04 Junior: Academic All-Big Ten selection. Saw action in every game of the season as a reserve. Contributed with solid post defense and rebounding. Averaged 8.9 minutes per game. Scored season-high nine points and had seven rebounds in NCAA Tournament first-round victory over Murray State. Had six points and five rebounds in Big Ten Tournament semifinal win over Michigan .

2002-03 Redshirt: Transferred to Illinois prior to the beginning of the 2002-03 school year and sat out the season per NCAA transfer rules.

AT TULSA

Originally recruited to Tulsa by former UI coach Bill Self. Lettered two years at Tulsa, playing in 71 games with 11 starts. Had career averages of 3.7 points and 3.0 rebounds over his two seasons at Tulsa. Averaged 4.4 points and 3.5 rebounds in 2002, while playing over 13 minutes per contest.

HIGH SCHOOL

Four-year letterwinner at John Marshall High School. Started both his junior and senior seasons while leading his team to a cumulative 42-26 record in those two seasons. Had career averages of 18.0 points and 9.0 rebounds. Scored at a 22.0 clip and grabbed 11.0

rebounds during his senior season. Shot 72 percent from the field and 35 percent from 3-point range as a senior. Earned First-Team All-District honors both his junior and senior seasons.

Shaun Pruitt

Born	Nov. 22, 1985
Class	Freshman
Position	Forward
Height/weight	6-8, 245
Hometown	Aurora, Ill.
Major	Liberal Arts and Sciences

HIGH SCHOOL

Illinois Mr. Basketball runner-up in 2004. Considered the top big man in the state of Illinois. Led West Aurora to tie school record with 32 wins and third-place finish at Class AA state tournament, averaging 16.5 points, 8.5 rebounds, 4 blocks, 2 assists and 2 steals per game. Led Blackhawks with game highs of 21 points and nine rebounds in win over two-time state champion Peoria Central and star Shaun Livingston in front of capacity crow of 8,200, including 24 NBA scouts. First-Team All-State by the Associated Press, IBCA and Chicago Tribune. Aurora Beacon News Player of the Year Second-Team All-State by the Chicago Sun-Times. Consensus national top 75 player as a senior.

Illinois Season Box Score (as of Feb 23, 2005)

RECORD	OVERALL	HOME	AWAY	NEUTRAL
ALL GAMES	(28-0)	(14-0)	(8-0)	(6-0)
CONFERENCE	(14-0)	(7-0)	(7-0)	(0-0)
NON-CONFERENCE	(14-0)	(7-0)	(1-0)	(6-0)

## Player	GP-GS	Min	Avg	FG-FGA	Pct	3FG-FGA	Pct	FT-FTA	Pct	Off	Def	Tot	Avg	PF	FO	A	TO	Blk	Stl	Pts	Avg
04 Head, Luther	28-28	911	32.5	157-313	.502	81-188	.431	64-78	.821	19	87	106	3.8	38	0	103	45	4	51	459	16.4
11 Brown, Dee	28-28	888	31.7	136-252	.540	72-154	.468	42-53	.792	16	59	75	2.7	54	1	134	51	1	55	38	613.8
05 Williams, Deron	28-28	926	33.1	128-300	.427	49-135	.363	45-66	.682	13	86	99	3.5	55	0	189	83	7	27	350	12.5
43 Powell, Jr., Roger	28-28	688	24.6	133-232	.573	13-35	.371	68-93	.731	60	82	142	5.1	75	0	9	23	7	18	347	12.4
40 Augustine, James	28-28	732	26.1	105-166	.633	0-0	.000	73-93	.785	75	123	198	7.1	60	1	37	32	38	25	283	10.1
50 Ingram, Jack	28-0	395	14.1	41-89	.461	6-13	.462	17-20	.850	35	44	79	2.8	49	1	14	11	16	11	105	3.8
45 Smith, Nick	28-0	335	12.0	44-110	.400	3-9	.333	14-21	.667	17	50	67	2.4	42	0	21	17	16	11	105	3.8
33 McBride, Rich	27-0	448	16.6	28-82	.341	24-73	.329	4-4	1.000	12	29	41	1.5	30	0	23	13	2	12	84	3.1
41 Carter, Warren	22-0	182	8.3	28-55	.509	1-4	.250	6-13	.462	15	25	40	1.8	21	0	2	11	5	7	63	2.9
55 Pruitt, Shaun	18-0	84	4.7	9-24	.375	0-0	.000	9-17	.529	10	7	17	0.9	15	0	0	10	1	3	27	1.5
34 Nkemdi, Fred	16-0	36	2.3	6-7	.857	0-0	.000	0-1	.000	4	1	5	0.3	5	0	2	2	1	0	12	0.8
TEAM										32	40	72	2.6	03							
Total	28	5625		815-1630	.500	249-611	.408	342-459	.745	308	633	941	33.6	444	3	534	301	98	220	2221	79.3
Opponents	28	5625		628-1481	.424	169-452	.374	294-449	.655	288	555	843	30.1	430	-	344	434	63	130	1719	61.4

SCORE BY PERIODS	1st	2nd	OT	Total
Illinois	1177	1036	8	2221
Opponents	820	896	3	1719

Illinois Combined Team Statistics (as of Feb 23, 2005)

RECORD	OVERALL	HOME	AWAY	NEUTRAL
ALL GAMES	(28-0)	(14-0)	(8-0)	(6-0)
CONFERENCE	(14-0)	(7-0)	(7-0)	(0-0)
NON-CONFERENCE	(14-0)	(7-0)	(1-0)	(6-0)

DATE	OPPONENT	W/L	SCORE	ATTEND
11/19/04	DELAWARE STATE	W	87-67	16618
11/21/04	FLORIDA A&M	W	91-60	15518
11/24/04	OAKLAND UNIVERSITY	W	85-54	13932
11/27/04	vs Gonzaga	W	89-72	14183
12/01/04	WAKE FOREST	W	91-73	16618
12/04/04	vs Arkansas	W	72-60	13140
12/06/04	CHICAGO STATE	W	78-59	16618
12/09/04	at Georgetown	W	74-59	12401
12/11/04	vs Oregon	W	83-66	21224
12/19/04	VALPARAISO	W	93-56	16618
12/22/04	vs Missouri	W	70-64	22153
12/27/04	LONGWOOD	W	105-79	16618
12/30/04	vs Northwestern State	W	69-51	2500
12/31/04	vs Cincinnati	W	67-45	2500
*01/05/05	OHIO STATE	W	84-65	16618
*01/08/05	at Purdue	W	68-59	14123
*01/12/05	PENN STATE	W	90-64	16618
*01/15/05	at Northwestern	W	78-66	8117
*01/20/05	IOWA	W OT	73-68	16618
*01/25/05	at Wisconsin	W	75-65	17142
*01/29/05	MINNESOTA	W	89-66	16694
*02/01/05	at Michigan State	W	81-68	14759
*02/06/05	INDIANA	W	60-47	16618
*02/08/05	at Michigan	W	57-51	13751
*02/12/05	WISCONSIN	W	70-59	16865
*02/16/05	at Penn State	W	83-63	10966
*02/19/05	at Iowa	W	75-65	15500
*02/23/05	NORTHWESTERN	W	84-48	16618

#	SUMMARY	GP-GS	Min	FG%	3PT%	FT%	R/G	A/G	STL	BLK	PTS/G
04	Head, Luther	28-28	32.5	.502	.431	.821	3.8	3.7	51	4	16.4
11	Brown, Dee	28-28	31.7	.540	.468	.792	2.7	4.8	55	1	13.8
05	Williams, Deron	28-28	33.1	.427	.363	.682	3.5	6.8	27	7	12.5
43	Powell, Jr., Roger	28-28	24.6	.573	.371	.731	5.1	0.3	18	7	12.4
40	Augustine, James	28-28	26.1	.633	.000	.785	7.1	1.3	25	38	10.1
50	Ingram, Jack	28-0	14.1	.461	.462	.850	2.8	0.5	11	16	3.8
45	Smith, Nick	28-0	12.0	.400	.333	.667	2.4	0.8	11	16	3.8
33	McBride, Rich	27-0	16.6	.341	.329	1.000	1.5	0.9	12	2	3.1
41	Carter, Warren	22-0	8.3	.509	.250	.462	1.8	0.1	7	5	2.9
55	Pruitt, Shaun	18-0	4.7	.375	.000	.529	0.9	0.0	3	1	1.5
34	Nkemdi, Fred	16-0	2.3	.857	.000	.000	0.3	0.1	0	1	0.8
Total		28		.500	.408	.745	33.6	19.1	220	98	79.3
Opponents		28		.424	.374	.655	30.1	12.3	130	63	61.4

100 Year Celebration

More than 350 members of previous Illinois basketball teams pose for a group photo after a postgame ceremony for celebrating 100 years of Fighting Illini basketball after the Big Ten basketball game between Minnesota and Illinois in Assembly Hall on Saturday, January 29, 2005.

The First 50 Years of Illini Basketball

A century of basketball. A CENTURY. That's how long they've been playing men's collegiate basketball in the state of Illinois. Well, at least in Champaign at the University of Illinois that is.

No, the hoops lineage in Champaign doesn't start with the likes of Nick Anderson, Kenny Battle and Kendall Gill and rest currently with Dee Brown, Luther Head and Deron Williams. Aside from all the hoopla surrounding the current squad, this season also marks the 100th anniversary of the University of Illinois men's basketball program. A century of Illini Basketball was celebrated that January weekend and head coach Bruce Weber figured he'd have some links to the past have a chat with his squad. Future Phoenix Suns and Arizona Diamondbacks owner Jerry Colangelo was an honorable mention all-Big Ten selection for the Illini in 1961.

Jan. 12, 1906 marked the first contest in school history as the Illini dismantled Champaign High School 71-4 (OK, so there weren't a lot of local college teams playing hoops at the beginning of the 20th Century.). Illinois, the University of Chicago, the University of Michigan, the University of Minnesota, Northwestern University, Purdue University and the University of Wisconsin formed the basis then for what is now known as the Big Ten Conference.

The Illini went through four coaches in their first four seasons, but by the time the next decade rolled around, the program was ready to start the winning ways that still continue today. Illinois finished its first full decade with a 95-48 record that included a 15-0 record and a national championship in 1915. Coach Roy Jones' squad grabbed what would be the first of numerous Big Ten Championships, including a second crown in 1917. Guard Ray Woods was a three-time All-American from

1915-17, the first Illini player to win such an award.

More success followed in the '20s as coach J. Craig Ruby's squad shared a league title with Wisconsin in 1924. Jones' 14-year stint as the head man is the third longest tenure in school history.

On Dec. 12, 1925, Illinois defeated Butler 23-22 in their new home. Huff Hall is named for longtime Illinois athletic director and coach George Huff. Huff served as Illinois' athletic director from 1901-35, during a time in which Fighting Illini athletic programs enjoyed unparalleled success. Huff served as the driving force behind the construction of Memorial Stadium. He also served as football coach from 1895-99, and baseball skipper from 1896-1919. Known by many of his close friends and business associates as "G," Huff served as manager of the Boston Red Sox in 1907.

Illinois athletics enjoy a proud tradition in Huff Hall. Huff Hall served as home for Illinois basketball from 1925-63, during which time the Fighting Illini won 339 out of 418 games (.811), eight Big Ten championships and earned two NCAA Final Four appearances. The Illinois basketball team played to capacity crowds for many years at Huff Hall, and fans often waited several years to obtain tickets.

Huff Hall was also the longtime home of the Illinois High School Association state basketball tournament, creating the circus-like atmosphere that fostered the term "March Madness." Huff Hall served as host for the 1991 Big Ten Women's and 1992 Big Ten Men's Gymnastics Championship, the 1993 NCAA Men's Gymnastics East Regional, a 1994 NCAA first-round volleyball match, a 1995 NCAA second-round volleyball match, the 1995 Men's and Women's Big Ten Gymnastics Championships and the first and second rounds of the

100

ILLINOIS BASKETBALL
CENTENNIAL

1906 2005

I

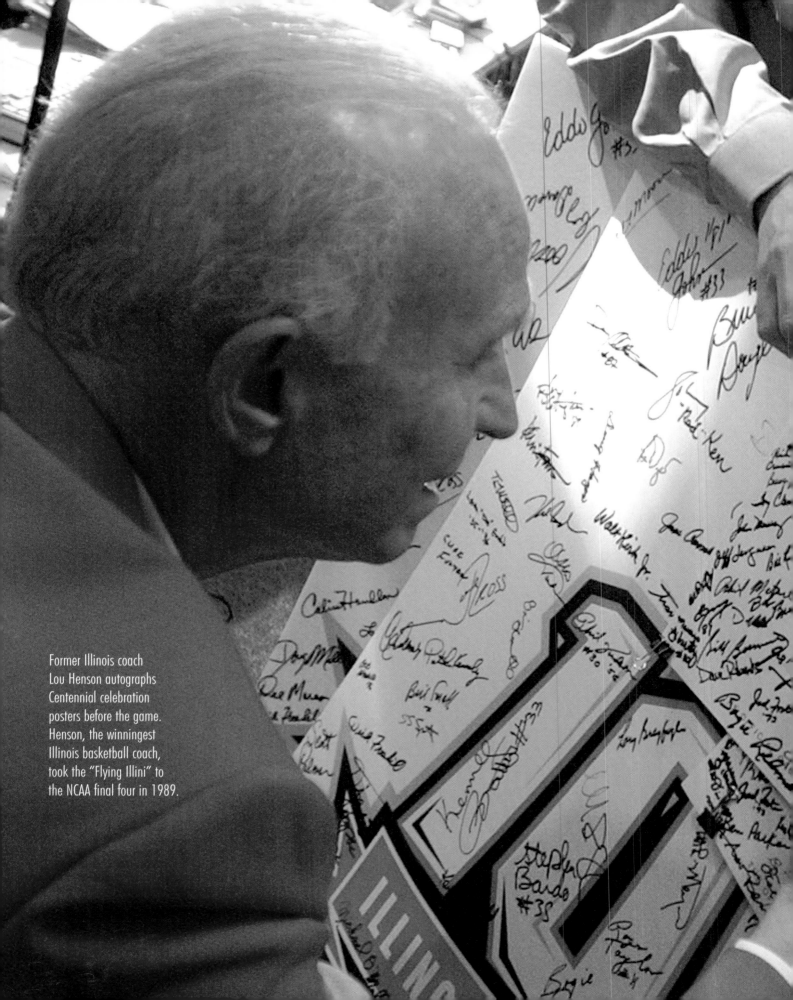

Former Illinois coach Lou Henson autographs Centennial celebration posters before the game. Henson, the winningest Illinois basketball coach, took the "Flying Illini" to the NCAA final four in 1989.

©AP Wideworld Photos

1997 NCAA Women's Basketball Tournament.

Constructed in 1925 at a cost of $772,000, the New Gymnasium was renamed Huff Hall in 1937 following the longtime athletic director's death.

The '30s brought Harry Combes, a three-year letterman that led the Illini to Big Ten championships in 1935 and 1937 (Combes actually came back to coach the Illini in 1948).

Coach Douglas Mills began his 11-year career with a share of the Big Title in 1936-37 with a team that was led in scoring by Lou Boudreau. Boudreau was an All-American for the Illini in 1938. He went on to a Hall-of-Fame professional baseball career which included winning a World Series and being named Most Valuable Player as player-manager with the Cleveland Indians in 1948 before spending a long career in the broadcast booth with the Chicago Cubs after various coaching stints. He was elected to the baseball Hall of Fame in 1970.

The Whiz Kids came to prominence in the '40s. Art Mathisen, Jack Smiley, Andy Phillip, Gene Vance and

Ken Menke won consecutive Big Ten titles with a combined record of 35-6 before all went into active duty in World War II.

The group returned from military service in 1947 and stepped on to the court at Huff Gym against Cornell on Dec. 6, 1946. The group played the first half in an 87-39 triumph. For his accomplishments, Phillips was elected to the Naismith Basketball Hall of Fame.

Combs took over the reigns shortly thereafter and won the first of his four league titles in the 1948-49 season. That season marked the school's first 20-win (21-4) campaign since 1908 and a third-place finish in the national tournament. The Illini won another league crown two years later and they finished third again after losing to Kentucky in the semifinals for the second time in three years.

The Illini finished their first four-plus decades with some impressive results. An undefeated season, trips to the national semifinals, countless Big Ten titles.

The second half of the century provided more highs than lows and produces numerous stars and superstars that shone brightly as the game of college basketball – and basketball in general – exploded into the popular pastime it is today.

(left) Nick Weatherspoon, left an Illini from 1971-1973, talks with Ken Norman, an Illini from 1985-1987, during the postgame ceremony for Illinois' Celebration of 100 years of Fighting Illini Basketball. Both were named to the twenty member Illini All-Century Team. (right) James Augustine comes out of the tunnel during the postgame ceremony.

Former Illinois basketball coaches, from left, Gene Bartow, Harv Schmidt and Lou Henson talk to the media before the game between Minnesota and Illinois. The three men represent 29 years of coaching at Illinois.

Illini Basketball – The Second Half of the Century

The University of Illinois men's basketball teams have been filled with famous and not so famous characters over the years. What is undeniable, however, is the Illini have succeeded more often than failed. In this 100-year celebration of Illini basketball, the second half of the century bears this out. Success was followed by some lean times before the Blue and Orange returned to prominence.

Unless you're really getting up there in years (no offense, heh, heh), you might only think of current Chicago Bulls TV color commentator Johnny "Red" Kerr as just the grandfatherly, cheerleading announcer that used to constantly scream over the top of the calls by play-by-play men Jim Durham, Neil Funk and Tom Dore during the Bulls' heyday of the 1990s.

Well, he's got a bit of history with the game here in the state of Illinois besides just rooting for his beloved Bulls. He hit the hardwood for the Blue and Orange of Illinois for the 1952 season after a stellar career at Tilden High School in Chicago. The Illini finished third nationally the year prior to Kerr's arrival. His first squad came within three points of reaching the national title game as St. John's tipped the Illini 61-59 in what is acknowledged as the NCAA's first official Final Four. The Illini closed the affair in Seattle with another third-place finish after beating Santa Clara 67-64 behind Kerr's 26 points.

Kerr finished his Illini career as the school's all-time leading scorer before he went on to a 12-year professional career, mostly with the Syracuse Nationals. He was also the first coach of the expansion Bulls in 1967 and earned Coach of the Year honors that season. Once again he is on the ballot of the Naismith Hall of Fame, and Illini Nation and Bulls fans alike are hoping this is the year he gets the call for all his contributions to the game.

Another highlight of the '50s saw the Illini snap the 51-game winning streak of San Francisco with a 62-33 throttling on Dec. 17, 1956.

Dave Downey rested the career scoring mark from Kerr in 1963 and that year marked the unveiling of Assembly Hall. The Illini stopped Northwestern 79-73 before 16,137 fans on March 4 in what is now the current Illini homecourt.

Illinois set a then-NCAA record by selling out all 11 of its home contests in 1970. This was during a downtime for Illini basketball, but that was about to change with the arrival of coach Lou Henson at the start of the 1975-76 season. By his fourth season, Henson's squad finished 19-11 including a win over top-ranked Michigan State and some kid named Earvin Johnson in 1979. Eddie Johnson_s winning baseline jumper at the final horn sent the Assembly Hall denizens into a frenzy and the Illini to a No. 2 ranking. Unfortunately, injuries derailed Illinois' magic ride as the squad slumped to 19-11.

The following season Johnson and Mark Smith led the Illini to a 20-win campaign and third place in the NIT. A year later Johnson and Smith were joined by freshman Derek Harper and the Illini went to the NCAA tournament after another 20-win campaign. Johnson and Harper soon joined the professional ranks as the NBA exploded in popularity and both enjoyed productive careers with numerous teams through the '90s.

In 1983 Harper was joined by the likes of Bruce Douglas, Doug Altenberger and Efrem Winters to send the school past the 1,000 career win mark with a win

Former NBA star Kendall Gill (Illinois 1987-1990) was named to the Illini All-Century Team.

over Texas A & M at the Great Alaska Shootout. With Harper gone to the Dallas Mavericks the following season, the Illini didn_t miss a beat. They finished 26-5 overall and 15-3 in league play which earned them a share of the Big Ten crown with Purdue. Henson also notched his 400th career coaching win that season. In the NCAA tournament, Illinois electrified the country with a run to the regional final where Kentucky secured a 54-51 win on its home court. You want to know why teams don't get to play on their home courts during March Madness? Point to this game. The NCAA changed its policy after the outcry from this contest.

The Illini opened the next year as the preseason No. 1 pick by some publications and reached the NCAA's Sweet Sixteen. By 1987, Anderson, Steven Bardo, Gill and Larry Smith took the Illini to another 20-win campaign but a first-round loss to Austin Peay (Austin Peay?) in the first round of the NCAA tournament derailed any hopes of any postseason magic.

Henson picked up his 500th win in 1988 with Battle and Lowell Hamilton added to the mix, but that was just setting the table for what would be arguably the finest season in Illini history — up to now.

Freshman Marcus Liberty joined the most talented Illini cast to that point, and the team took off — literally. The Flying Illini electrified fans across the country with fast-break basketball, high-flying dunks and all-out tenacity and enthusiasm. Illinois ran off 16 wins to start the season and reached the top of the mountain with a No. 1 ranking after a December victory over Georgia Tech. Gill's broken foot delivered a severe blow to the Illini, but the squad regrouped and finished second in the Big Ten and secured a No. 1 seed in the NCAA tournament.

Gill returned to the lineup and Illinois opened the tournament with wins over McNeese State and Ball State at the Hoosier Dome before heading to the regional final in Minneapolis. The Illini powered past Louisville and Syracuse to reach the Final Four in Seattle. And who was in their way? Good ol' conference foe Michigan, which the Illini handled twice during the regular season. Three was not the charm as Michigan came out on top and went on to defeat Seton Hall for the National Championship.

The Flying Illini set season records for points (3,110),

steals (341) and wins (31) all the while giving fans memories which last to this day. The group is considered by many as the best in Illinois history. Anderson and Gill each spent more than a decade in the NBA, while Bardo, Battle and Liberty also all reached the NBA as well. Was this the most talented team in school history? Quite possibly.

After the oh-so-close run from the Flying Illini, the program found itself scuffling its way through the early 1990s. Oh sure, there were the occasional NCAA and NIT appearances, but there was also a losing record for the first time in 14 years. It was time for Henson to take the Lou-Do out to pasture after the 1995-96 season. In 21 seasons at the helm, Henson recorded 423 victories with 11 NCAA tournament appearances and 11 20-win seasons.

Lon Kruger took Florida to a Final Four in 1994 and he was tabbed to succeed Henson on the Illini bench. He took his first Illinois squad to the second round of the NCAA tournament and recorded a 22-10 mark. That was the highest win total by a rookie Illinois coach to that point. Kiwane Garris finished that season second on the career scoring list with 1,948 points and set records for free throws attempted and made while finishing second in the conference scoring race with a 19.4 average.

Kruger took the Illini to a share of the league title in 1997-98 and the team moved into a new practice facility under his watch. Additionally, Kruger and athletic director Ron Guenther saw to it that Assembly Hall stands were moved much closer to the court to give the team more of a home-court advantage.

On the court, the Illini entered the 1999 Big Ten tournament as an 11th seed after a rough regular season but made an amazing run before losing the title contest to Michigan State at the United Center. The Illini reached the NCAA tournament for the third time in four seasons under Kruger in 1999-2000 led by Cory Bradford, a second team all-Big Ten selection after setting the school mark of 96 3-pointers made.

Soon after, Kruger was off chasing the riches of the NBA's Atlanta Hawks, and the Illini were in search of their 15th head coach. Enter Bill Self, who came to Champaign after leading Tulsa to a 32-5 mark and a spot in the regional finals in 2000.

Former NBA star Eddie Johnson (Illinois 1978-1981) waves to the crowd as he is introduced as part of the Illini All-Century Team.

Frank Williams (Illinois 2000-2002) was named to the Illini All-Century Team.

Deon Thomas (Illinois 1991-1994) was named to the Illini All-Century Team.

With the likes of first Frank Williams, Marcus Griffin and Brian Cook, followed by Sean Harrington, Brian Johnson, Robert Archibald and Damir Krupalija, to Williams and Brown, Self was the toast of the town with two Big Ten Championships, a run to the Elite Eight and a run to the Sweet Sixteen in just three seasons. But after just three seasons, Self was plain toast to the Illini faithful as he left for Kansas University when Roy Williams left there to take the post at the University of North Carolina.

Fortunately for Guenther and Illini Basketball, Bruce Weber was available after a sterling five-year run at Southern Illinois University, and he has maintained the tradition of Illinois success started some 100 years ago.

The second century of Illini basketball has had just as promising a start as the first. Stay tuned . . .

Here is a list of the All-Time University of Illinois men's basketball team, as selected by an online vote:

Ray Woods (1915-17)

Chuck Carney (1920-22)

Andy Phillip (1942-43, Œ47)

Gene Vance (1942-43, Œ47)

Dwight "Dike" Eddleman (1947-49)

John "Red" Kerr (1952-54)

Dave Downey (1961-63)

Duane "Skip" Thoren (1963-65)

Don Freeman (1964-66)

Nick Weatherspoon (1971-73)

Eddie Johnson (1978-81)

Derek Harper (1981-83

Bruce Douglas (1983-86)

Ken Norman (1985-87)

Kenny Battle (1988-89)

Nick Anderson (1988-89)

Kendall Gill (1987-90)

Deon Thomas (1991-94)

Frank Williams (2000-02)

Brian Cook (2000-03).

Brian Cook (Illinois 2000-2003) was named to the Illini All-Century Team.

Quotables

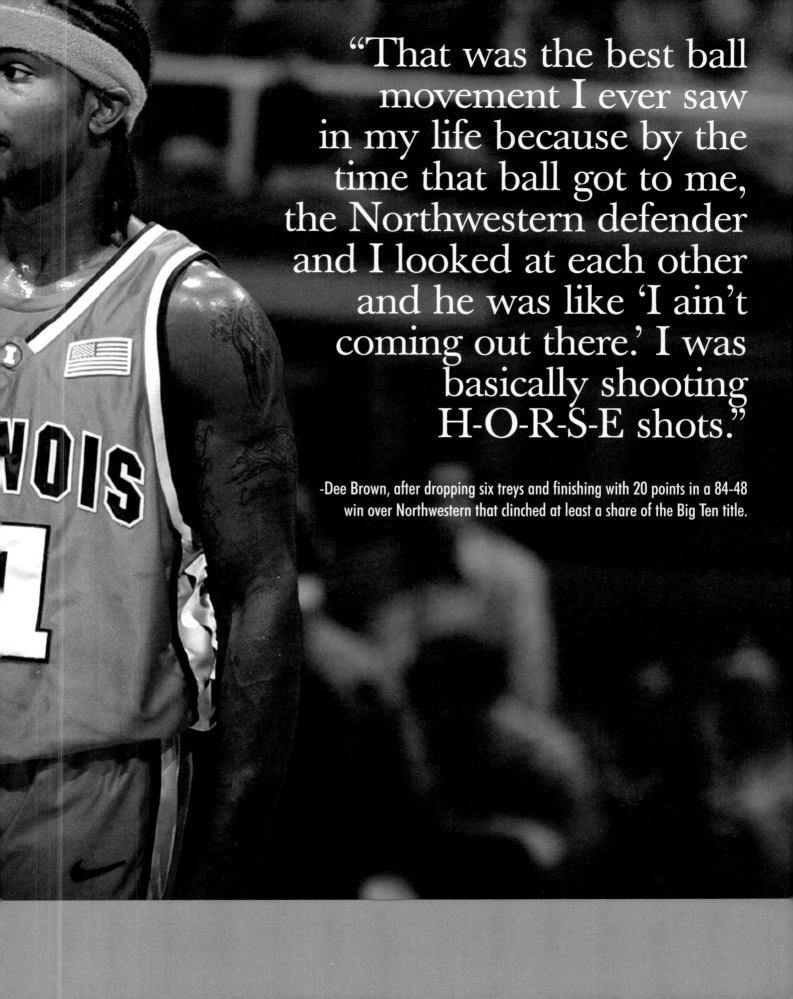

"That was the best ball movement I ever saw in my life because by the time that ball got to me, the Northwestern defender and I looked at each other and he was like 'I ain't coming out there.' I was basically shooting H-O-R-S-E shots."

-Dee Brown, after dropping six treys and finishing with 20 points in a 84-48 win over Northwestern that clinched at least a share of the Big Ten title.

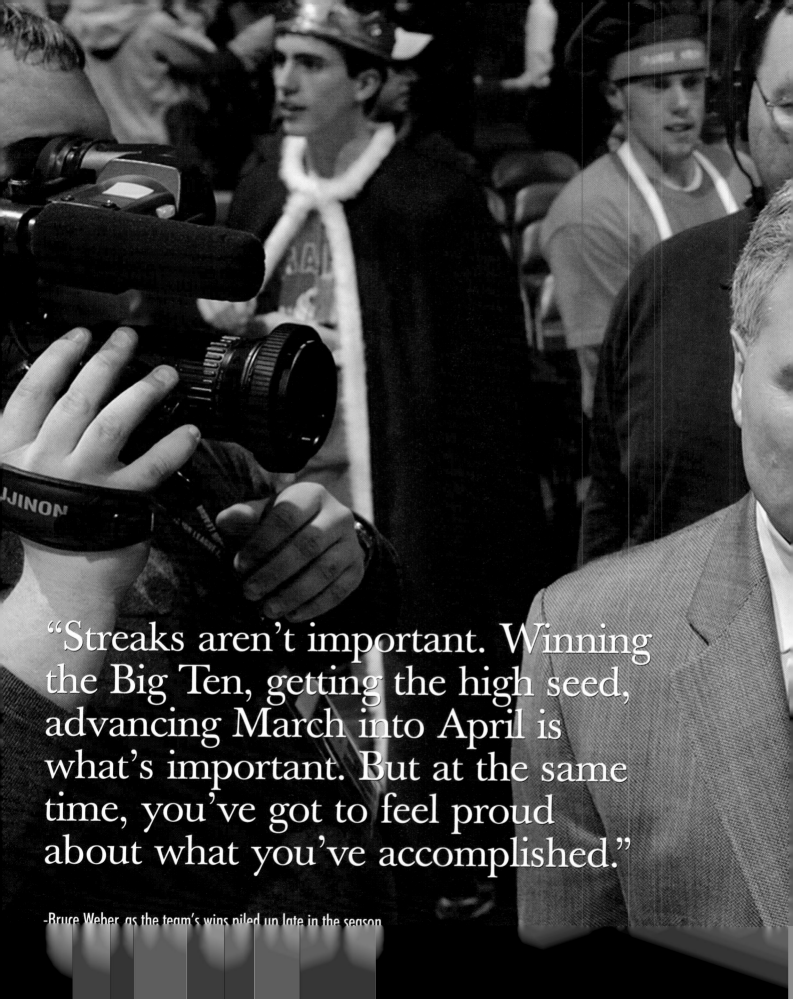

"Streaks aren't important. Winning the Big Ten, getting the high seed, advancing March into April is what's important. But at the same time, you've got to feel proud about what you've accomplished."

-Bruce Weber, as the team's wins piled up late in the season.

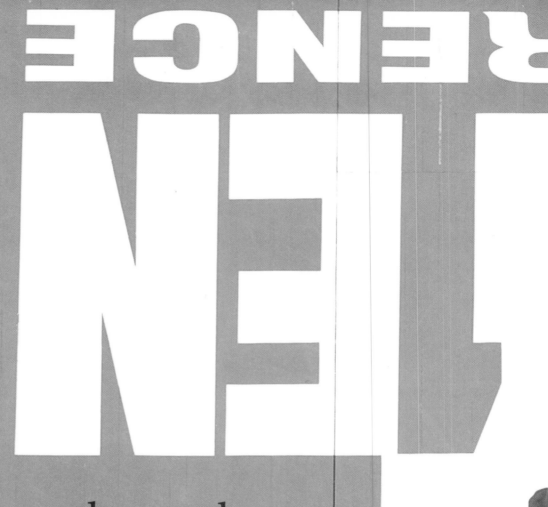

"It was good to make some baskets, but the guards set me up,"

-A typically humble Roger Powell Jr., after going 10 for 10 from the field and scoring 21 points in a 83-63 win over Penn State

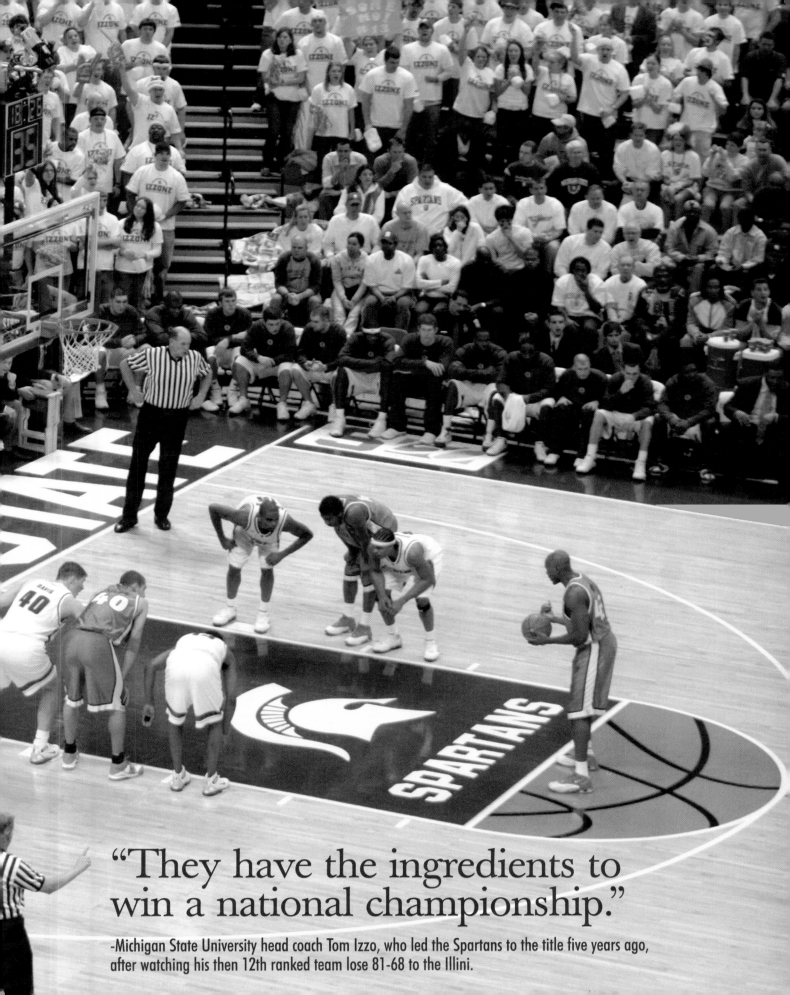

"They have the ingredients to win a national championship."

-Michigan State University head coach Tom Izzo, who led the Spartans to the title five years ago, after watching his then 12th ranked team lose 81-68 to the Illini.

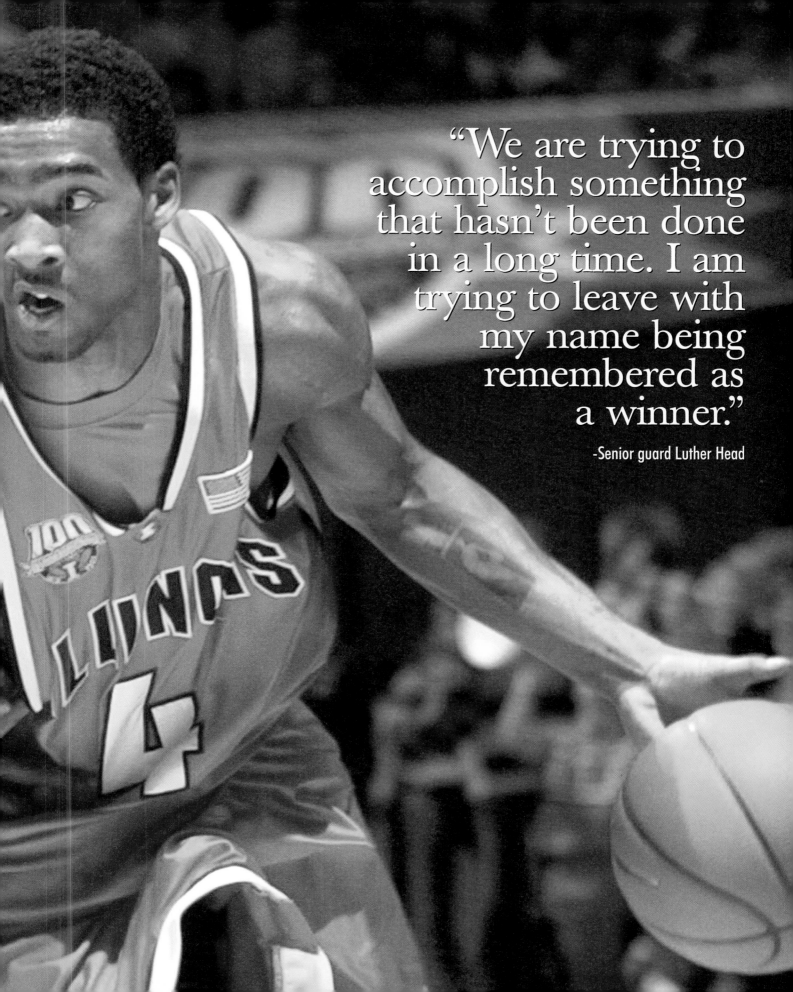

"We are trying to accomplish something that hasn't been done in a long time. I am trying to leave with my name being remembered as a winner."

-Senior guard Luther Head

"It was a surprise,
but we played great,"

-Coach Bruce Weber, after 5th ranked Illinois annihilated the #1 ranked Wake Forest Demon Deacons 91-73 in the ACC-Big Ten Challenge. The Illini led by as many as 32 points in the second half.

"In 1989, I remember labeling Illinois as the Flyin Illini, with coach Lou Henson (or Loo Doo) guiding a super team: Kenny Battle, Marcus Liberty, Kendall Gill, Stephen Bardo, Lowell Hamilton. This year's team is special too – the Flyin Illini Part 2, baby! Illinois is an offensive machine that plays tough defense too. The fans in Champaign in Orange Crush country have something to smile about."

-ESPN analyst Dick Vitale

"I'd love to win every game by 20, but that's hard. We needed to win a game like this."

- Deron Williams, who scored nine of his 19 points in the final 3:19 to help the Illini overcome foul problems, poor shooting and a late run by the Tigers to beat Missouri in St. Louis, 70-64.

"His teams play tough defense, and play the game the right way."

-Purdue Coach Gene Keady, Bruce Weber's mentor and friend for 18 years, where Weber was his No. 1 assistant coach.

"Good team, good players - they find a way to make plays. They don't feel the pressure. I think they're as good as anyone in the country."

-Iowa coach Steve Alford

Orange Krush: The Fans